I AM NOT A STEREOTYPE I AM H.E.R.

Dr. Pamela Gurley, D.M.

Clark and Hill Enterprise

This edition brings new stories and insights, including a chapter updating my journey of love and trust, fresh reflections on resilience, the power of sisterhood, and more. These additions are a testament to how we continue to grow, heal, and redefine ourselves...together.

admin@clarkandhillenterprise.com

Elkridge, Maryland 21075

Second Printing

ISBN 979-8-9990790-3-9

eBook ISBN 979-8-9990790-4-6

Audio Book 979-8-9990790-5-3

Printed in the United States of America

Contents

Dedication

To my love, Julius C. Clark, III. You were not my husband when this first came out. But here we are... intertwined 4ever! Thank you for continually supporting my dreams, encouraging my visions, and showing me every day what it means to be loved organically.

To my mother, Pamela Jones. Thank you for your unwavering support. You have always set the best example of authenticity in how you present yourself to the world. I love you infinitely.

To my dad, Ronald Gaskin. Thank you for doing what many men would not do and doing so unselfishly. I am a better woman because of it.

To my sisters, Rolonda Rooney and Robin Wynn. You both have taught me the meaning of life, the value of patience, and the power of laughter. Thank you for making me an amazing auntie.

To Lil Joey, Pierce, Drury, Jasmyne, Olivia, Dooby, Malik, Jordyn, Zoe, and Pamela. My legacy and all I do is for all of you.

Message from a Friend

I met this feisty little lady about 7 years ago when we worked at the same agency. My first thought was that this woman is spicy and a handful. She must be a Scorpio. (lol) Little did I know that we would form a sisterhood and lifelong friendship. I look up to her like a big sister and value her advice.

Watching her determination and fullness of life pushes me to be a better woman and person in this world. She really lives unapologetically, and it is beautiful to watch. Her heart is so pure and warm, and she amazes me with all she has accomplished. She is bold, doesn't hold her tongue, and yet so lovable. Her love for her family and friends is commendable, and I'm so glad to be a part of her journey, cheering for her on the sidelines. She has taken me on adventures I never knew I'd enjoy, and

I look forward to more experiences in years to come. I truly believe there is nothing she can't do. Everything she dreams of comes true because of her beliefs and detailed plans. I am honored to be her friend.

This book is another venture for Pam, and I am excited for the world to get a glimpse inside of a phenomenal woman, my sister, and my friend, Dr. Pamela Gurley!

I love you, and words cannot fully explain the joy I have for you.

- Tasani Butcher

Foreword

Choosing to own your life, having the courage to reveal
who you really are, and embracing your vulnerabilities
without guilt or shame is not a path for the faint of heart!
— Marquita Herald

Anyone who really knows Dr. Pamela Gurley (affectionately re-
ferred to as "Pammy Pam" or "Ms. Pam" by her 6:23 MARC
Penn Line train family) knows that she does not shy away from challenges. Over the years, I, along with other members of her train family,
have witnessed her incredible tenacity and grit as we celebrated and
shared in her numerous professional achievements: promotions, com-

pleting her Doctorate, launching a business of which she is the CEO, producing a podcast series, coordinating, and embarking on a women's entrepreneur speaking tour, and so many others. All of this while traveling across the globe to exotic and faraway countries and islands.

So, none of us were surprised that she was authoring a book. However, given everything I have written thus far, I think everyone will be surprised to learn what motivated her to write this book. That is because anyone looking in from the outside has seen exactly what Ms. Pam wanted you to see...the picture she painted for you...in the hopes that she would "fit in" and be accepted in a world in which she feels constantly judged because of her physical features. Although cliché, everything isn't always as it seems...or is it?

In this book, she opens up and is very transparent about her struggles in life to gain self-love and self-acceptance, which have made her vulnerable to abusive and unhealthy relationships. Ms. Pam's life journey is a case study on how one's life experiences—how people perceive us and treat us—significantly impact our behaviors, positively and negatively. She proved me wrong (and right)! As a diversity practitioner, I pride myself on enthusiastically encouraging people to temporarily "suspend judgment" by consciously allowing themselves a minute to take in more information and view things through the best interpretation possible before drawing a final conclusion about people, especially based on limited encounters with them.

I know that we can never deeply understand someone-- in particular, why they behave the way they do and see the world the way they do--without knowing their backstory. However, I must admit that I myself have fallen short of following my own teachings, especially when it came to judging Ms. Pam.

Just like so many other people that she has encountered throughout her life, I, too, negatively summed her up in 30 seconds when I met her. I'm human, so it was all based on what I saw on the surface. Just imagine this petite powerhouse prancing to the back of the train (where the 6:23 crew sits) with the confidence of a runway model in 6" stiletto heels, wearing a very fitted dress, and designer bags hanging off her arms. She possessed the physical features many black women have been socialized to desire and resent simultaneously—a melanin hue enough to know she clearly has African ancestry, but not too dark to be considered undesirable by Eurocentric beauty standards; long, thick, naturally curly "good hair;" and a small waist with a fit body. I took those observed facts and created a story. Hmph...who is this chick? She must be bougie. She must think she is gorgeous. Then, in that first encounter, she disclosed she had a Master's degree, was a military veteran, was accomplished in other areas, etc. Sadly, that only intensified the negative judgment. Little did we know Ms. Pam was dealing with internal struggles. As she shares in the book, "On the outside, I looked perfectly put together. I continued to push myself to excel academically and professionally, but internally, I was broken."

Just as Ms. Pam was taking her journey of self-discovery and self-acceptance, little did we know that we were on that journey with her. I am happy to say that shortly after meeting Pam, and even more, as I got to really know and understand her and become familiar with her life experiences, I realized that she embodies and is unapologetic about all the things I initially judged her to be. She is vain. She is pretty. She is accomplished. She is ambitious. She is also human and, at times, deals with self-doubt and insecurities. She is the personification of her book's title, "I am not a stereotype...I am H.E.R."

Her journey and everything about her scream, "I will not allow you to put me in a box!" I will not allow you to dismiss me or oversimplify who I am. I am not a stereotype...I am HER! Welcome to her journey. It will teach all of us something about prematurely judging others and what happens when we succumb to external pressures to live our lives based on how others will perceive or react to us, versus being and loving all pieces of our authentic selves, whether they love it or hate it.

~ Tinisha L. Agramonte

Preface

At every age, there is an internal conflict in how we see ourselves. While I am grateful to have not had a childhood booming in an age of social media, I can very much relate to some of the adversities of it. It took me a long time to decide if this book was worth writing, and while I see there are many dynamic books about color barriers and conflict, they do not necessarily reflect my experience. They also do not reflect my perspective, and I owed it to myself to let my voice be heard. After all, I can only speak my truth.

Naturally, writing a book about the way the world sees women of color, I could only have written through the lens of being a lighter shade of brown and being born in an era before technology boomed and social media affected the way we live, the way we think, the way we interact, and the way we see ourselves and others as women. It is absolutely amazing the impact technology has on ego and self-esteem. I am also of the opinion that women of color have to work harder than most minorities and face increased stereotyping. The more educated, the more financially independent, and the more career-oriented we become. It affects the confidence we feel within (imposter syndrome), our personal relationships, and our failure to tear down the walls of imperfect insecurity.

I Am Not A Stereotype: I am HER is my way of breaking the mold in the way the world sees and regards shades of melanin. It is breaking the mold of excuses that are put on Black women to make them feel inferior. It is breaking the mold to set the example that melanin is beautiful, no matter what shade. It is breaking the mold for young women to love what made our ancestors rich in character and strong in will. Last, it is my journey, thoughts, and perceptions of being a driven, ambitious, melanin beauty growing beyond the stereotypes, adversities, and barriers placed before me. It is my view of the world we live in and how I have thrived and survived.

"Never compare yourself to others. We are all born unique and with our own stories. Love yours! Replication is falsification." - Dr. P. Gurley

Introduction

"A happy childhood is one of the best gifts every parent gives to their child. It is the world that tries to take it away." ~ Dr. P. Gurley

On Saturday, November 8, 1975, in a small town in Texas, I entered this world on a prayer and a promise. A promise that would test the faith, compassion, and honor of any man (especially a married one). This promise was also a decision that would test the resiliency of a family. It was a promise of the gift of happiness. You see, to my mom, that was all that mattered to her. Of course, not just for me, but for my older sister as well (who was a little over a year and a half old when I was born).

I also entered this world [according to my dad] in the most unusual fashion. Do you believe in angels? If not, my dad would certainly tell you they exist. Why? Because he said, I entered this world with a halo over my head. And, I know that may sound crazy as hell, but he swears he was not drunk or high when I was born (hello, it was the '70s). As a matter of fact, he was 100% certain that was what he saw, and when he saw it, he knew I was even more special. But how much more special could I have been to him? So special that he signed my birth certificate, knowing I was not biologically his.

You would think a situation so flawed would be enough to make any man walk away. But not my dad. In that situation, he said to my mom, "We all make mistakes..." The how or the why of their situation never mattered to me. The only thing that mattered was that he knew about me long before I came to be, and he was as present as my mother was when I entered this world (halo and all). Believe it or not, his decision set the tone for how I viewed human imperfection in others when I got older.

My earliest childhood memory is of my family, and I took a very long drive from Washington, D.C., to Southern California to take a flight to Hawaii. Why on earth would any parent want that level of torture with two toddlers is beyond me!! I was around 18 months old, and my sister (who was a little over 2 years old) and I were very energetic toddlers. I remember my dad constantly yelling at us to sit our asses down because we would run from one side of the back seat to the other, laughing and playing. This was back when seat belts were not a law required to be upheld.

Growing up in Hawaii until I was five years old was an experience (from the things I can remember about it). The experiences I cannot remember, I am able to see in old photographs. Can you imagine a childhood growing up on an island?! Well, if you lived near one as beautiful as the beaches in Hawaii, you could certainly understand the love for it. This probably explains why I was barefoot and wet in a lot of my pictures and why I loved going swimming so much.

Do you know what was so unique about the pictures I saw of every birthday party I had in Hawaii? I recognized they were always inclusive of many ethnicities. I cannot confirm or deny if that would have been the case growing up on the Mainland, but it was certainly noticeable when I saw pictures growing up in Hawaii.

Because it was so expensive to purchase airline tickets for a family of four (five after my sister, Robin, was born), we did not travel back to D.C. until my dad had a permanent change of duty station (PCS) to Georgia.

Both D.C. and Georgia are not only different from one another, but they were also very different from Hawaii in terms of relationships and censorship. Because we were not near extended family and living in a military community, there was far more diversity available to us. I don't know if my parents dealt with racial barriers in Hawaii, but if they did, they did a very good job of shielding us from them (and it never showed in any of the pictures from our time in Hawaii).

While I am sure it was nice returning to the Mainland, where we had family, I am equally sure it had to be a transition for us kids. It certainly was for me. Why? Because from the moment I returned, I was immediately made aware that my dad was not my dad and that I was different from my sisters. They also made it very clear I wasn't "from" D.C. because of my accent. This is a lot to process at six or seven years old, and believe it or not, I was not bothered by it, nor accepting of it. Call it denial or not, but it didn't feel like it was for me to have to deal with. I just wanted to enjoy my summers despite the constant interference from family and friends.

The man they "claimed" to be my father was absent. He would come around every blue moon and try to talk to me, filling my head with lies, so it made it very difficult for me to connect with him. Don't get me wrong, my mom did not hide details about his family from me. I actually spent time with his mom (my Nana) and his sisters (my aunts) when I visited D.C. during the summer (or the holidays if I were in the city). Again, all that mattered to her was for me to have a happy childhood because he (who I often refer to as the sperm donor) was an addict who spent most of his life in detention centers or in jail.

Even though I was young, mentally, and emotionally, I was able to compartmentalize those relationships and never let them interfere with my happiness. Did it affect my childhood? I honestly don't know how to answer that. I would like to think it did not. I have great memories of my childhood, traveling all over the United States with my mom and sisters, and spending summers and spring breaks with my grandmother and cousins. There was no "color" that was seen because, during my summers in D.C., I rarely saw white people where I grew up. And while I was in elementary school in Georgia, my friends and I were all "colorful" kids who wanted to have fun regardless of what we each looked like. Imagine that.

Part 1: My Journey

Chapter One

Victim of my skin

"Not one of us has perfection to offer, and we do NOT have the right to demand it from others." - Dr. Gurley

It was not until my pre-teen years that I realized just how much the world saw color (and judged that way). I know, crazy, right? I am not saying I was sheltered or ignorant of the fact that my skin was bursting with melanin; however, I was not raised to feel differently about it. For as far back as I can remember, I was exposed to diversity. I don't know how old you are, but if you grew up in the late 70's and early 80's, there were not many television stations that showed music videos, so my sisters and I watched artists like Prince, Michael Jackson, ZZ Top, Van Halen, David

Lee Roth, Madonna, Bananarama, David Bowie, Wham, Boy George, and more on Night Tracks (1983-1992) and Night Flight (1981-1988). This, of course, was also the very early years of MTV (1981-Present), but these shows aired late nights on weekends on other stations, and I do not recall them being 24-hour-a-day stations. I do distinctly remember that most stations aired rainbow-colored lines when the stations went off.

During that time, I cannot remember many Black syndicated television shows other than Good Times, Fat Albert, The Jeffersons, What's Happening, The Cosby Show, and Sanford and Son. Though these shows existed, my sisters and I watched popular shows like Facts of Life, Different Strokes, and Dukes of Hazzard (in which, I am sure, nearly every child back then tried jumping into the car through the window at least once when their parents weren't around), Happy Days, Knight Rider, Family Ties, Who's the Boss, Three's Company, and many, many, many more. What I am trying to say is that there were not as many shows showing people who looked like my sisters and me. Of course, by the late '80s, there were many changes, though, by this time, I fell in love with books (mostly romance novels) and still had a love for many of the shows that continued to lack the representation of Blacks characters. Let me just say that I did like Black television shows and tuned in, but naturally, there were not always a lot of them to watch. So, I gravitated to what was available when I wanted to watch television.

So, if you made it this far without passing judgment, then KUDOS! Because of the above-mentioned, I became exposed to racial stereotyping. Sadly, my awareness of my skin began with my own race. I distinctly remember it being when I attended my first junior high school dance (I am guessing around seventh grade or so). Of course, the school had to play every genre of music to accommodate everyone attending the dance, so there was no shortage of soft rock and alternative music mixed with hip-hop and "booty" music.

Let me pause to explain exactly what "booty music" was. In the late 1980s, South Florida music really began to hit the "map" (especially in the all across southeast area of the United States). It was all about the bass and raunchy music lyrics (though the clean version was played on the radio and at school dances). Songs like Poison Clan's Shake What Yo Mama Gave Ya, 69 Boyz's Tootsie Roll, Splash Packs' Scrub the Ground, and any 2 Live Crew songs were all a part of this new wave genre of southern "booty" music. OMG, just thinking of those songs makes me want to dance!!! I am so thankful to have grown up between Southeast Georgia and Washington, DC. It really exposed me to all genres of music.

Anyhow, like any other teen, I dressed to be "fly." It was the days of biker shorts/pants, and since my dad was stationed in Korea, my sisters and I had every brand and color with shoes in the same colors to match. I stepped out of the house ready to have fun and enjoy the time out with my friends. During much of the evening, I had to continuously explain to my friends and other schoolmates why I was able to sing nearly every song that came on, no matter what it was. Personally, I didn't think it was unusual not to. I'm just saying, if the music came on the radio, it was meant to be heard by all, not particular races. I still feel this way today (and yes, my genre of books, music, activities, and television shows continues to be diverse). It is very easy for such questions to be dismissed if asked once or twice, but that is not what happened. It was no longer a question asked but turned more into a light fare of consistent teasing.

By no means was I the type of girl who was easily intimidated by anyone. Sadly, being pretty can make you a target from other girls (who I assume did not think much of themselves or did not receive enough love or attention from their parents). I remember my first "the way I look" fight was in middle school (actually, it took place after school on my walk home) and was for no reason at all other than for being pretty. A girl considered to be a bully at my school pushed and pushed for me to fight her, all the while indicating how I thought I was all that and too cute, etc., etc. You know what, a fight is exactly what she got from me.

I blacked out in anger, pinned her against a tree, and all I remember was her cousins breaking it up. No, she did not win, nor did she get the upper hand, so she decided to come to school the next day with a knife intending to cut me on my face. No doubt anyone in my family would tell you my dad raised a fighter, but he also raised a smart young lady, too. So, I let the principal know of the threats told to me, and the girl was suspended for bringing a knife to school. Yes, she was mad and made more threats, but I refused to be bullied by some ugly-spirited girl. After all, I was really just starting to learn about myself and my emotions; I surely had no time for that shit.

As my teen years went by, I remember being told I "acted" white, talked white, was shaped like a white girl, and was often asked what I was mixed with. How does one even begin to process this as a teenager? Part of me didn't. One part of me constantly internalized why I was considered to be different; the other part of me refused to see "color" in ways that others did. Yes, I deliberately chose not to address it. I felt thankful I had sisters who were much like me in terms of loving diversity in all things, so it was easy to accept my character and personality as "normal." I also believe part of my psyche did not process this the way it probably should have.

Teenage years are already the hardest years because it is a time of self-discovery and learning acceptance. Acceptance of things you like about yourself, things you like about others, and acceptance of things you dislike or, dare I say, hate about yourself. And don't let puberty be unkind...you certainly need no outside influence to help you dislike yourself even more. Puberty is like fuel, and society is the flame. Let's face it, even before social media kids were not kind and often pointed out your flaws or picked with you because of it.

I know I will probably shock my older sister, Ro, when she reads this, but outside of the teenage acne puberty cursed her with, I felt like she was the lucky one. She was blessed with full lips, coarse hair, and hips. And then there I was...{deep breath}...thin lips, thick but curly hair, and no hips. Quite honestly, I was not too sure what to think of my features back then. I just spent so much time growing up wanting to be like her that by the time I was a pre-teen, there were far too many differences between us, and out the window went any form of mimicking. And the hair...I was just so envious of hers. She was able to get her hair pressed with the hot comb, and I was the most envious when she was allowed to get a jerry curl. AUGH, yes, I wanted a jerry curl so badly, but all my mother did was wet my hair and put some curling product in it, and it would curl right up. BORING!! It was such a disappointment, but I had to be happy with it if I wanted to have my hair like my big sister's. She also had the best clothes because she was much "fuller" in her hips than I was. I was so small that for the longest I could wear kids-size clothes even as a teenager (and to be honest, even at times as an adult in my late 30s). Gosh, I have the torturous memory of wearing a size 6x from age six until I was 8 or 9 years old. To further (and briefly) digress just a bit more, if you look at many of our early childhood pictures, I am emulating my older sister a lot (and we also dressed alike a lot.) My younger sister and I did, too, but we babied her quite a bit since she was the youngest. Not much to emulate there. Okay, so let me fast forward to where I was before my digressive rant.

By the time I graduated high school, the way I "looked" became more of an apparent reality for me. Light brown skin with "good," long hair, high cheekbones, petite, and "pretty" felt more like a curse than a blessing. Continuous external judgments do something to the psyche of a young woman's esteem, no matter how confident she may appear on the outside. It is truly the worst kind of victimization of one's appearance.

When you are trying to find yourself, it makes it very difficult to wrap your head around your imperfections and, at the same time, try to hold on to what you love about yourself (especially when everyone judges you or dislikes you for those very things). There was (and is) absolutely nothing more annoying than being asked the following: "Is that your hair?" "Where do you buy your hair from?" "What are you mixed with?" or "Can I feel your hair?" So many times, I wanted to just yell at these people to just leave me the fuck alone. It is just hair! Not only that, but everyone is born different, to be different, and to look different. Hello! That is what makes each of us unique. But uniqueness is often followed by discrimination and/or criticism (good, bad, or indifferent).

My first encounter with discrimination was at the age of 20 while a lifeguard and a private swim instructor at the YMCA in Buckhead, Ga. The memory is burned in my mind because it was a devastating blow to my self-esteem and psyche. I worked the early morning shift and was relieved each afternoon by a Caucasian, chunky, gay male each day. In the afternoon, after my lifeguard shift, I would provide private swimming lessons to clients who had been on a very long waitlist for $25 an hour. For a 20-year-old who did not have her first job until the age of 19, this was golden on top of my lifeguard pay. Well, it was apparently not so golden for the lifeguard who relieved me each day.

The problem started with my lifeguard swimsuit being a two-piece (which was not so common in 1995-96). I often alternated between two bikinis and one full-body swimsuit. Each time I worked in my bikini, he would make comments regarding my choice of swimsuit. I cannot remember the precise date or day, but after my morning shift, my manager called me into her office to talk to her before my private lesson began. Long story short, and to quote her exact words, she said, "...it is not your work ethic or job performance, but (insert chunky lifeguard's name) is not comfortable working with you, and therefore, we have to let you go." I was floored by this because all the patrons loved me; I had never been late, and I had always helped out when needed. But in all of this, I was fired because a White, gay man who had been working there longer and had a better relationship with the manager did not like the way I looked in a swimsuit, and it made him "uncomfortable." It was so utterly insulting and mind-blowing that I immediately went and filed an Equal Employment Opportunity (EEO) complaint against the YMCA.

In my mind, I wish I had stuck to it, but I dropped the case when I enlisted in the Army (I was not able to have any open cases of any kind before being sworn in). Unfortunately, since then, I have continued to face unnecessary discrimination from dark skinned women, obese women, skinny women, Caucasian women, Hispanic women, gay men, Black men, Caucasian men, and African women, all on the basis of my physical appearance. As you are reading this, I am sure you are wondering why all of the dislikes, questions, or speculations regarding my physical appearance. Believe me, I have been considered many things, but never do people think I am solely African American (which, in my opinion, I look very much so). But to share, ethnically, I am multiracial. I am African American, Mexican, and Native American Indian. Actually after doing a genetic ancestry composition test, I now know I am Sub-Saharan African, North American Indigenous, British, and Irish.

Just to note, it is not that I did not (and do not) recognize discrimination was (is) prevalent or the fact that people still have opinions regarding external features; I am just not a fan of being victimized because I do not "fit" a certain look to a particular person or group of people, or act a certain way that is not familiar or not "color" common within a stereotype. Quite honestly, the effects of these on a young woman who yearns to find herself, her career "placement" in life, and where she socially fits in are quite detrimental to her mental health. It certainly became a game of lost and found for me and it did not always feel good,

nor did I make the best decisions because of it.

Chapter Two

I Am Not Bitter

"Bitterness is the anchor that keeps us tethered to past pain, preventing us from sailing toward new possibilities. Letting go isn't about forgetting; it's about freeing ourselves to grow." – Dr. P. Gurley

There is a pretty big misconception that all black women are bitter. I can assure you that if a woman feels that particular way, it is purely circumstantial and often formed from losing herself while in (or coming out of) relationships. I am not stating that all relationships make a woman become "bitter bitches," but what I am stating is that there is often a root cause creating it. Women are emotional by nature, and relationships, especially intimate ones, have a way of making women lose themselves or question themselves. And even though she may seem bitter, it is mostly a defense mechanism to mask pain or guilt. I am not sure when I lost myself or at what point I began to feel lost, but I remember being in a string of unhealthy relationships, yearning to "fit" in and be loved for who I was (or who I thought I was). I [admittedly] settled far too often for what I thought was happiness or what I thought was logical for me to have. What was worse was that some of the relationships I was in were physically and/or mentally abusive or just outright toxic. I excused my behaviors and actions and blamed myself for the lies and cheating because I didn't look or act a certain way. I also compared myself to every woman I was cheated on with (because they did not look like me, did not speak like me, and did not act like me), and/or felt I was not "sufficiently" ingrained in the culture enough to understand what a black man needed. Or so I thought. For over a decade, I felt trapped in a body that was never "black" enough or was too "pretty" to have value or be valued.

Because my thoughts of myself were so toxic, I dated and/or married men who had issues with me making more money than them or being too ambitious. I also dated men who were intimidated by my ambition and/or my need to succeed. Being in a relationship was so taxing that I completely lost focus on my personal life and focused on my academic and professional life. It was definitely not the best way to think or go about my relationships.

First, But Not Last

High school should be a period in a girl's life where she feels free to create who she wants to become. I was never that girl. I never felt a need to fit in, and it showed in my friendships with other girls. Don't get me wrong, I had LOTS of friends and acquaintances. I was also well-known in my school. In my 10th-grade year, I started dating a guy who had graduated my freshman year (he was a senior when I was a freshman). I was sixteen and he was nineteen (it was not an issue like it is now), and I liked that he was not in school (as I don't really recall dating many boys my age). I think my first high school boyfriend was 18, and we dated for a few months before breaking up because he cheated on me with his ex-girlfriend. Even at that time, it was not easy for me to put my heart into many of my relationships. Back then, I felt the highest amount of love I could have for anyone was my mother. I didn't really know love like I knew friendship between two people. There was love, and then there was being in love. I had a difficult time with the being in love part. I dated the same guy for eight years, so I had no real experience in relationships. In the beginning, it was really great. He spoiled me rotten. There was nothing I could not have and nothing that I didn't get. I turned down getting my car for my 16th birthday from my parents because I was not allowed to work, but I also never had to worry about transportation because he let me drive his car. I was young and naïve, and since I had never had a serious boyfriend before him, I made his "kindness" into forgiveness. If he did anything wrong, we went shopping. I accepted that as an apology. This went on for years, not realizing this was a red flag. Once I graduated, he changed even more, and not for the better.

We had been together for just over two years when I graduated. I think it was difficult for him to fathom me no longer having a curfew. I can now go out and be out as late as I want. He became insecure and jealous, even though he had been going out and hanging out late from the time we began dating. It was hard for me to wrap my head around this change at 18 years old. I didn't make those insecurities better by dating other men. Oh, YES, I dated other men while we were together. A part of me felt as though I wanted to give him a reason to break up with me because I didn't want to be the one to blame for breaking up.

The summer after I graduated, I moved four hours away to attend Columbus College (now Columbus State University), and he never came to visit. He actually only came one time, but that was to pick me up to take me back to my mom's for a weekend because my car broke down, and I wanted to go home. Of course, I was surprised he did so, but then again, not so much considering he was not staying in Columbus.

While in my first year of college, I took a lifeguard course, which became my first job, so finding a summer job at home was easy. Our relationship that summer was not. He would show up at my job unexpectedly, accusing me of cheating with patrons who swam there. He did not like it if he saw me talking to any man (old or young) who was only asking about the swimming classes, water aerobics, or swim team information for their kids. Are you kidding me? I am at work!!

At the end of the summer, I didn't return to Columbus because I was offered a job in Buckhead, Atlanta, as a lifeguard and swim instructor. So, I moved and transferred to DeKalb College. Though I was four hours away from home again, he had never come to visit me. Do you know what that is like? I will tell you...FREEDOM to do as I please. And that I did. Our relationship became an on-again, off-again situation after a while. I admittedly went back because I was used to him, and I think it was probably the same for him.

I got tired of attending college, so I moved back home for a while. I also knew that if I didn't want to go back to school, I would be removed from my dad's medical insurance. So, I did what many people do who want to do something better for themselves—I join the military. I shared what I wanted to do with him, and he told me that if I joined, it was over. Okay! I was not the kind of girl you give an ultimatum to, so I enlisted, and off I went!

My time in the military was short but a hell of a lot of fun despite the medical issues I began to have shortly after arriving at Fort Hood (technically, they started a few months before while I was in Fort Sam Houston). Long story short, I ended up honorably discharged and medically retired for asthma, and as soon as I moved back home, my high school sweetheart and I reconnected. He told me he had changed, and for a while, he did. Because we were living together, there was a lot of pressure from people for us to get married. After all, we had been "together" for eight years, and we were in the South, where most people did not date for so long before tying the knot. So, we did. And from there, our relationship went from not okay to just fucking awful. I went back to college and worked on and off depending on my school schedule. I had strong pursuits for education, so in several of our arguments, he would say, "If you wanted to be with an educated nigga, you needed to leave and go be with one." Why would that even matter? It was as if he had an issue with me wanting to better myself. Was I supposed to only sit at home and cater to him? We didn't have children, so why on earth was education and me always working a damn issue? But it always was.

I worked as a front desk manager at a hotel for a short time, and he would pop up, accusing me of cheating. How? I was taking 5-7 classes each semester AND working. When in the hell would I have time for that? We began to argue a lot and over the most menial things. But also, the reality was that he was cheating. How do I know? Because the woman he was messing with called our house and asked, "Who is this?" I let her know I was his wife! He was working a swing shift and sometimes worked at night. I called him and then told him I was calling her on 3-way. Before she could open her mouth, he said, "Shine, my wife is on the phone. Why are you calling me at my house?" Oh, now, that is guilt right there! I was so angry that I broke dishes on the kitchen floor, so it would not be easy for him to make it to the bedroom. From there on, it just went downhill like a sled on an icy hill.

We were very different from how we used to be, and most of all, I think it was because I was far more progressive than he was. I wanted to travel, do new things, and try new foods. He was fine going to work and coming home. We went out, but it was mostly to eat and go to the movies. Life became boring, especially after I graduated from college.

I think we both came to realize neither of us was happy. I started buying things here and there and packing them in boxes. By this time, I had decided to start graduate school. It was tough because at that time I was not working at all. Thankfully, I had very little financial debt and was receiving a retirement check, so it helped out with the small household bills I had. I moved out, got my own place, and within 3 months had started working on a military base as a Program Educator.

For a while, he would pop up unannounced, asking who was in my house. I was done, we were done; why was he at my house? We went about two years separated, and when I could afford half, I asked him to meet me at the divorce lawyer's office to sign the papers. And just like that, it was over. I am not going to act like I didn't have a life while we were separated. Life had moved on for me as soon as I moved out of the house we shared.

I was in a "situationship" with a man for over a year (which ended because of our differences in what we each wanted). He wanted to treat me like a girlfriend, but not actually have me as one, and that did not fly with me. Our relationship was interestingly toxic. I say that because I deliberately would make his life hell at times to push him away, and he would not leave me alone. We loved one another as friends but could never move forward with anything more. He deployed, leaving me with some of his stuff to look after. As a friend, I did just that, but still chose to move on with my life.

Second Chance at Nothing

There was not much time between my divorce from my first husband, my relationship with Mr. Situationship, and my marriage to my second husband. As a matter of fact, as petty as it sounds (and to be honest with myself), I married my second husband to spite him. Yeah, I know...a totally screwed up, petty, and extremely toxic way of thinking!! As you see, I am not afraid of putting my truth out there. It is what it is. Here again, and as I said previously, I put my education and career first and, in those areas, I was soaring!! My second husband and I met through work. He was a military police investigator, and from the moment he met me, he was smitten. He often asked an older black gentleman he worked with, named Mr. Roberson, about me and told him to let me know he had a crush on me. After that, it was not long before we went to lunch, became friends, and then moved in together after around month three of dating.

Living together was interesting. He was scared to take me to his hometown to meet his parents, but was equally scared to have his parents visit us. He grew up in Coco, Florida, and was as redneck as they come. Crazy, right?! But it worked. When his parents came to visit, they ended up loving me. And from then on, life was "normal." He had a daughter who lived in the same town, so she spent nights often. He and the daughter's mother had a six-month, six-month agreement, so she lived with us on and off (eventually living with us when her mother relocated to Colorado with her husband who was military).

We only dated for around six months before getting married. The funny thing about our "wedding moon" was that I told him, "Let's not do this. Let's treat this like a vacation. No one will know whether we got married or not." He became emotional and started to break down (crying). It made me cave, and on Catalina Island, we wed. Not every day in our marriage was terrible. We actually had some really good times. He was attentive, and it was easy to travel together. If I were having a bad day at work, he would send me flowers to me at work or have flowers waiting for me at home. We just naturally got along. But eventually, his insecurities would manifest and turn what had the potential to work into a living hell.

There were times in our marriage when he became so insecure that it became extremely concerning. If I talked about leaving him, he would put a gun to into mouth and threaten to kill himself. Or become erratic and manic. He drank a lot and took a lot of pain pills (prescribed for his back problems) to cope with his feelings. He often told me he did not care how miserable he got; he was not leaving me. What the fuck!!? Many of my friends were very concerned, so for a short while, I moved out.

It was difficult being in an interracial marriage. On the one hand, Black men often stared at me with what I felt was disappointment or disbelief (some even shared their negative opinions on it or questioned me about "why" I would marry outside of my race). On the other hand, I had a husband who had a difficult time with my race and was very insecure because of it. His insecurities brought out the worst in him, and where he fell short, I made excuses for him. I outright dressed up my marriage to look perfect because I felt so guilty about my decision to marry. Guilty for dating outside of my race. Guilty for making excuses for the racist comments said in my presence (and trust me I spoke up about it). Guilty for not listening to my gut instinct when I said to him, "Let's not get married..." Guilty for marrying him to spite another man. Just outright guilty. Guilt, when not dealt with, can make for an ugly bedfellow.

While we were together, he often told me he did not see me as Black. Why? Because being light-complexioned, proper (in language and how I carried myself), graduate degree educated, financially "put together," etc., made me regarded "less than as a nigger." Actually, what I was told (for further elaboration) was that there were Blacks, and then there were niggers, and there was a difference between the two. I apparently did not fit the bill of a "nigger" because of the qualities I previously mentioned. This is exactly how it was explained to me. Of course, it was no secret; I was not white or regarded as such. He had even told his daughter she better not ever bring a Black man home. I guess what was good for him was not good for his daughter.

Despite my unhappiness, I tried to make it work. After all, I made the decision to marry even though I was not in love (which was something he knew). We went to marital therapy, and he told the therapist, "I am not used to being with someone so pretty that other men want her," and that I must "miss Black dick" because I was with him, a White man. In my mind, I thought," This cannot really be happening to me?" Seriously?!

But it was. This was my reality. There was no way I would ever be happy with someone so insecure. So, I just lived. That did not make things any better, and actually, it made it worse.

His insecurity about my making more money than him is what ended our marriage. He took a job in El Centro, California had the promotion potential over the course of 3 years. He had known about it for months, but shared it with me two or three weeks before it was time for him to report. We lived in southeast Georgia, had a kid in school, and owned our home. You don't just make a decision to move across the country with no plan. Well, I wanted to make sure HE went, so I put the house on the market and had a buyer in 3 days. We sent his daughter to live in Colorado with her mom. I moved into a condo in Brunswick and he drove to California with our dog thinking I would join him in a month or so. That did not happen. I had visited a few times, and he had returned to visit the East Coast when his mother passed, but by then our marriage was essentially over. At least for me, I was done! And a few months after the death of his mom, I mailed him divorce papers (after being married just over five years).

Third Time Was NOT a Charm

My third husband and I met through a mutual acquaintance at a birthday dinner. I won't say we immediately hit it off, but we did exchange numbers and spoke quite a bit. I had shared my experiences openly with him from my previous two marriages, personal things about my life, and how, if I were ever to be in a relationship again, I would rather date a man who did not have children. I was also open about being separated but had not filed for divorce yet because I didn't want to do it so soon while my then-second husband grieved the death of his mother (I am not that insensitive). He, in return, shared things about himself. He told me about his career in the military (being deployed a lot) and that it was the reason he had never been married or had children. He deployed a lot before we had met, so that was a completely understandable reason. Eventually, we developed a relationship, and a few months into our relationship, my divorce became final.

Our dating was fun, loving, confusing, crazy, and outright toxic. In my mind, I thought I knew what I wanted. I thought I was ready to deal with my heart now (which was not always so easy to do). Honestly, I was so mentally detached most of the time in the past that it was easy to walk away. But this time, I thought I had struck gold and had found the one who accepted me for me. The truth was that I overlooked all of the toxic behavior shown to me and my behavior in response to it. Sadly, the only reason for this was my own state of mind. I was broken. I was toxic. I thought because he was an officer in the military, getting his Master's degree, and had a nice body (he lived in the gym) that he would be my equal and not insecure over how I looked, how ambitious I was, or feel some kind of way because of my personal successes. Boy, was I wrong! He was quite manipulative. When we argued, or I said I was done, he would take things of mine as a reason to be in touch with me. He even went as far as stealing clothes from my suitcase one time and then threatened to throw them away. I told him to do so, and I would buy them again. Of course, he apologized for his actions, and we were good again. We did this rollercoaster ride for most of our dating. My friends and family tried to warn me, but I was blinded by my own toxicity. And when he did show me who he was, I ignored or made excuses for it. Clearly, you can see how damaged I was. When he proposed before leaving for Kuwait, I said yes. I honestly don't know how or why in the hell we stayed engaged the first eight months he was in Kuwait. We were good on some days and horrible on others. And those horrible days were really bad ones, even though we were in two different countries.

After a year and a half of dating, we decided to get married during his temporary break home to make it easier for me to be on his orders to Germany (instead of afterward). I honestly feel neither of us even wanted to, and I'm not sure why we even did. Hindsight is a bitch, and a late one at that. Just before we married, he was on the balcony of my apartment on the phone. I went out and asked if he was okay. He began to explain that he had just found out he had a daughter, and he knew how I felt about being with someone with kids. He said his dad sent him the information while he was in Kuwait. I said to him, "You would have to get to know her, just like I would." We talked more about it and his feelings about it before going to get married.

This marriage broke me in a way that I was not mentally prepared for. He was a great soldier, but a horrible husband and an extremely toxic man. Seven months into our marriage, my entire life changed, and I was too far from home to undo things, so I thought it would be better to try to make it work. When we moved into military housing, I found a written note that read, "I think about killing her in her sleep." When I first confronted him about it, he was cocky about it. When I called his Command because I did not feel safe, he lied and said it was from a movie. YEAH, RIGHT! I certainly valued my life enough not to just let this pass or think I could feel safe. He was removed from our home the day after our household goods arrived, and while unpacking, I found the mother-load.

Inside the fireproof safe where he put our documents, I found not one, but TWO divorce decrees AND a child paternity test dated 2001 (we got married in 2009). Remember, he told me he had never been married. He also told me he didn't have kids when we met and that he had just found out about her just before we married. To add insult to injury, BOTH of his divorces were due to cruel and inhumane treatment!!! WTF!! No wonder he wrote on our marriage certificate that he had zero marriages!! You are required to provide proof of divorce if you have been married before.

During the short time we were married, I endured a lot of mental, emotional, and physical abuse. I endured heavy criticism and judgment from personal things I shared (he didn't know I found the documents until about a month after I found them and made a comment as snarky remark to his criticism), how I looked, and how I acted. I lost friendships, damaged relationships, and distanced myself from people I was close to. All for a person whose life was a lie and who was not worth it. I was cheated on, lied to, threatened, and blatantly disrespected. He even hated me for being close to his family because they exposed the truth in the lies he told me.

We had several physical fights, with some resulting in black eyes, my hair pulled out, my head slammed on the floor, a drink thrown in my face for no reason at all, and what I am sure were bruised or fractured ribs. I was even spat on one time because I caught him cheating and broke his phone during a physical altercation. And yes, I had him arrested.

Let me explain how toxic I was. I had him removed from the home in Germany and arrested in Virginia, and each time, like many domestic violence victims, I recanted my story. My reason was not always because I thought I loved him, but because I felt he was dangerous. A man who loses the career that he loves has nothing to live for. Especially him!!! He was more toxic than I was because I feel he never got the therapy he needed from all of the deployments he endured. Yes, I am a firm believer that PTSD is alive and real, especially when you "slip through the cracks" and do not get the treatment you need.

After a really bad physical altercation one night, I left. What made me leave this time? I knew I needed to leave this relationship because I wanted to take his life as he slept in a drunken stupor. I was in Germany, and we lived on the "economy" (off-base). I am not the jail type, especially in another country!! So, I left with no words while he slept. How I left was interesting, and what I felt could only be God's work. A female called his phone, and I picked up. I had spoken to her earlier when he locked me out of the house because I had taken his phone. She was concerned and relieved I had picked up and not him. She said she could hear the things going on in the background and felt my life was in danger. She also said that from the time they met, she knew something was off about him, so she declined to see him or take an interest. I told her I was going to leave in the morning, but she said she couldn't rest knowing I was there until then. I had already bought myself a plane ticket, so I packed my things, and she came to pick me up. I stayed at a complete stranger's house until morning when she took me to the airport. I remember sitting at the airport in disbelief, wondering how in the hell I got to this point in my life. I knew then I needed to make better decisions for myself and for my life. He called and texted as I sat in the airport. He accused me of cheating and asked who the man was who picked me up from his house. He still has no idea how I left (well, maybe now, if he should ever read this). Oddly, our signed divorce papers were with a lawyer (on hold), but I made sure they were on hold no more (he also made sure of that, too).

I left the marriage not asking for anything. I just wanted out. And that is what I got...OUT!

Needless to say, after my third failed and unhealthy marriage, I took a much-needed break for self-discovery. There were so many unhealthy feelings I had about myself because I constantly compared myself to other women who looked different from me. I never cared about what they had because education, employment, and financial security I had always had. I seriously wondered what made them so different from me that men I dated and/or married felt the need to cheat (no matter how good I was to them or how much sex we had). I also wondered why I was regarded as less than Black because of how I naturally was (person-ality-wise, character-wise, and in things I liked). Don't get me wrong, I LOVED who I was...just not most of the time. Yes, I can actually admit I had a problem in this area (even though the people I dated and/or married probably thought of me as vain at times). And let me just say, it is tiring to hear, "I was the one that got away," after the realization sets in that the grass was not as green on the other side (after the breakup). I no longer believed in apologies, only actions.

Nearly a year after our divorce, my ex-husband (#3) tried to come back into my life. He claimed he had changed. But guess what? So had I. I was not the person who was married to him, and I certainly was not the person I was when I left him, and I would never be that person again. I knew it would not work, but I still gave him the benefit of the doubt. He didn't last 60 days. I was completely okay with that. I continued on with my consistently happy life. And the way I set my life up, not one of my exes could ever have another chance, especially the last one. I didn't care if he returned to me with Jesus on his back, begging for his forgiveness. He is forever a HELL NO! The door is closed because my mind is healthy, as is my spirit.

Despite the past, I have no anger or animosity with any of my exes (though one is deceased now). We aren't friends, but I don't consider any of them enemies either. Forgiveness and acceptance of "self" changed my perception and the way I wanted to live. I also did not want to give energy to Bitter. Bitter meant caring, but in a toxic way. Bitter meant I had residual feelings that lingered. Bitter meant I was still toxic...and I no longer was.

Chapter Three

The Pedestal Philosophy

In the darkest days, when I feel inadequate, unloved, and
unworthy, I remember whose daughter I am, and I straight-
en my crown." – Unknown

I want to begin by getting into the depths of the pedestal philosophy.
You see, this is my own philosophy without regard to research or
fact. It is simply about a personal observation through the journey of my
life experiences. I believe once you understand the logic and perspective
behind it, you will find it holds a deeper meaning than what is on the
surface. You see, everyone, at some point in their life, desires to be on
someone's pedestal; however, they neglect to place themselves on their

own. Is there value in doing this? YES! When you love yourself and place yourself on YOUR pedestal, you only have expectations for yourself. You make your world about you. This may seem a little selfish, but how can it be? Think of it this way: what is healthy self-love? It is placing your comfort before anyone else's. Is that not what life is about...being comfortable? Being comfortable is being internally happy. And I mean genuine, authentic happiness. Truly listening to your spirit (or your "gut") holds more value for your self-esteem and self-worth than anything else. It begins here. It is not losing yourself in someone else's desires, opinions, perceptions, and/or wants for you. You are able to truly "take care of you" and make the right decisions for you (after all, it is YOUR life). In doing this, you are able to take care of others. It makes you a better listener, a better friend, a better mother, and a better lover, wife, and/or companion. It is where balance meets authenticity.

If you ask yourself the question, "What am I worth?" there should be a laundry list of good things. This list should have all things intangible, but certainly not necessarily be exclusive. Do you have those things in your life? If the answer is no, what is holding you back? Whose life are you living? Are you fulfilled? If you were or are on YOUR own pedestal, you will be able to answer all of those questions with clarity, or at least acknowledge the truth in your responses of why you do not have them.

The journey of life is beautiful (even through pain). I can speak from experience about joy, pain, truth, perseverance, living for someone else, losing myself in someone, ignoring the red flags, and so much more. And now, my pedestal is my own. No one else sits there or will ever sit there other than me. It does not make me untouchable, not feel hurt/pain, or unapproachable; however, it does give me an inner calm to know that no matter what life throws at me or who walks away, life will go on, and my happiness will continue.

Raw and uncut, let me explain why you should no longer want to be on someone else's pedestal...it is unhealthy! Why? It is the breeding ground of toxic relationships. After the newness of a relationship wears off and reality sets in, things change (for better or for worse). Have you ever gotten to a place in a relationship where you lose yourself? Where, no matter what you do, it is never right, so you make even more of an effort to please (even outside of your comfort zone)? A relationship where you are never praised or appreciated for your good deeds but are often criticized for the bad ones? And to be more direct, any poor decision (even with the best and most humble intentions) is always the center of many arguments (even weeks or months later). The worst part is ALL of this comes from an IMPERFECT person. And because of the imperfections of this person, it is easier to have you on their pedestal and criticize than to put themselves there and have to hold themselves to all of the unrealistic standards they have for you (normally due to their internal insecurities). No one can possibly expect to be honest (or true) to someone else when they cannot be honest or true to themselves. Calling all oxymorons!!

The state of authenticity requires a person to feel validated within. It is not about the external world. It is about YOU! It is about loving yourself enough to sit on your pedestal. It is never wrong, yet we often allow ourselves to be influenced by external factors that prevent us from putting ourselves or keeping ourselves there. The fact of the matter is, self-love is an individual process. Note, I said process. It is not a naturally occurring practice. It takes work every single day to want to live by our own expectations and not expect others to do the same.

I also want to stress there is a difference between being authentic and loving oneself. To be authentic is to know yourself, be genuinely true, and accept all things concerning you. Self-love is favoring your joy, happiness, and comfort over someone else's. This does not imply you will not compromise; however, the decisions you make are ones with your values, respect, comfort, and esteem remaining intact.

Love vs. Self

There is nothing more special than the "earlyhood" of dating. The butterflies, the anticipation, the nervousness, the anxiety over what to wear, what to say, and what to do keep your mind cluttered for days, weeks, and sometimes months. We desire to be wanted, to be needed, and to be cherished. We desire to be the first thought when someone wakes and their last thought before going to bed. After all, it is what we do when we are attracted to someone. Therefore, we naturally want "our place" to be the same. But where (or what) is that "place" exactly? That place is the position of unequivocal admiration, also what I call the "pedestal." What is it about the pedestal that is so endearing that we fight to get there? While I could answer that, I am going to let that stand on its own and allow you (the reader) to answer that for yourself.

There is one period in life that is necessary for personal growth to occur. I could have said there are many; however, I believe there is only one moment in life where you lose yourself and find it very difficult to bounce back. It is the period between the break-up and finding yourself. There is something about that time that is the hardest (that is, if you have really loved someone to the point of losing yourself for the sake of wanting to keep the relationship). It is the point where you feel hopeless, depressed, angry, confused, and uncertain. It is also the period when you are most vulnerable and needy (yes, I said needy, and this is why so many people find it easy to rebound). I, too, have been guilty of that in the past (of course, this was when I was not in love and simply bored from one relationship to the next). When I thought I fell in love, it was different. I ignored all the red flags, overlooked the toxicity of the relationship, and did everything I could to please him (not realizing I was just as unhappy with myself as he was with himself). I forgave because I thought it was the right thing to do, and no matter how he treated me, I tried to make it work. No matter how much he lied to me, cheated on me, and verbally & physically abused me, I forgave him with every apology. As I said before, I prayed a lot before the separation, and I prayed a lot before the divorce. Then one day, something hit me. I listened to my spirit, and all of a sudden, there was something blocking me from staying or going back. I let go of what I realized was unchanging, unhealthy, and toxic. When I decided to take a break from relationships and focus on myself. Let me tell you, it was the HARDEST period of my life.

Facing Painful Realities

On the outside, I looked perfectly put together. I continued to push myself to excel academically and professionally, but internally, I was broken. It is amazing what an appearance you can paint for the perception of others!! I had traveled a lot, gone out a lot, and spent a great deal of time with family and friends; all the while, I was broken on the inside and hurting. Thankfully, I wanted to be free and followed my spirit about not involving myself in any romantic relationship. After about a month of my internal pity party, I decided to change my outlook and FINALLY be honest with myself. Divorce can make you feel like a failure, but it was the truth about it that set me free. Why do we not divorce our feelings when the divorce is final? Why do we continue to think about what we could have done better? Why do we carry the baggage of blame? So, the first thing I did was let go of the "I was wrong," "it was my fault," "I should not have walked away a long time ago," "I should have fought harder," and finally placed the blame where it needed to be...on him. After all, I was not the only one in this marriage. I was not perfect, but I was a damn good wife. I had made excuses for him long enough, and that truth set me free. I took responsibility for my life and divorced the emotional baggage I was carrying. I also decided not to date or have sex with anyone until I resolved the emotional feelings I had for my ex and began to love myself again. Denial is a bitch, and there is nothing wrong with having feelings after separation or divorce. It is natural!! Actually, the faster I admitted, "I am not completely over my ex," the faster I got over him! When I made that small but necessary mental shift, I went through a series of emotions. I was at least no longer depressed, bitter, or angry. I was no longer a victim of my own internal misery either. But now I was faced with "so, what now?" and that was where I was met with new feelings and emotions.

Climbing on My Pedestal

I wish there were a lost and found for personal growth. It most certainly would have made my journey to self-love much easier. Where in the hell do you begin to answer the question, "So, what now"? I had gone from depressed to angry to being confused. WTH? Emotionally, I was all over the place. For the record, it is a very odd place to have it completely together academically and professionally, yet be a straight-up hot, toxic mess personally. As I stated, I am only keeping it real. Nothing has ever destroyed my will to be successful or excel in meeting every milestone I planned for my life. God protected me in that regard, but apparently, he worked me a little harder on finding the authentic me through self-love. I figured the best thing to do was to see things mentally, emotionally, and truthfully for what they were. So, I decided to make two lists. One list was composed of what I wanted to do or enjoyed (and it was composed without fears, or money, or any other tangible or external factors). The second list was composed of qualities I bring to a relationship. I know the latter may seem a little strange; however, I have learned that much of what I give is those things I would like (at a minimum) to have reciprocated (pedestal qualities). Through the second list, I also gained insight into who I was and what I deserved. What I learned from the first list surprised me, though.

My first list was composed of many things that taught me about my strengths, my weaknesses, what I feared, and what I truly liked. It was composed of things I realized I enjoyed but stopped doing because it was not enjoyable to the person I was in a relationship with. Or things I wanted to try that were not an option because I felt the need to do it with someone instead of being okay with doing it alone. Granted, I learned to love my own company before I was married; however, the truth was I restricted myself because I did not want to cause further insecurities to the person I was with, which were due to his actions and not mine (a red flag I ignored before marriage and during our marriage). All in all, the first list taught me who I was outside of others. I then took that list and introduced those things to my life. I made a dedicated decision for myself for that.

And my, oh my, the second list taught me how to place myself on my own pedestal. It taught me who I was and who I wanted to be. Everything on my list made me know what I was worthy of and what not to settle for. What I want you to understand is that my list consisted of substance qualities and not the superficiality society pushes upon us (whether subliminally or upfront). If you compose a list of your own qualities, you cannot set your expectations so high for others. Never ask for things you are not willing to give yourself. This keeps you balanced and keeps you humble. If you see yourself as a self-respected woman, you will not settle for less than being respected. Why be good to yourself and allow someone else to treat you badly? Be honest in assessing your own qualities. And if there are qualities you desire, work at gaining them. Keep in mind, self-love is a process. You WILL have to work outside of your comfort zone to achieve it. This is easier when you are not distracted by external factors.

When I titled this particular chapter, it was because when I discovered who I was, I realized the truth did not hurt at all and that my anger was internal. It made me stronger. It made me more aware. It made me more intentional. It made me honest about who I was and who I wanted to be. It evoked a more profound passion of love for me. The truth made me grow, and growth is a positive way forward. Growth means you are not stagnant or complacent. Growth means you are actually living and not allowing life to pass you by because of circumstances or situations. Growth means you have given up idle thoughts of "what if" and have moved to "I am glad I tried."

Now it is your turn. Go forth, compose your list, and create the life you want for yourself. After all, no one can live your life but you. Never be ashamed of who you are, at the mercy of a closed mind. LIVE your life. LOVE your life. EMBRACE your life. LIVE your TRUTH. That is what it means to sit on YOUR pedestal!! And what a huge difference it will make, especially when it comes to love!

Chapter Four

Not "Settling" For Him

If you EVER want to know what HAPPY feels like, fall in
love with yourself. Then & ONLY then can love follow. –
Dr. P. Gurley

W hen you are happy with yourself and live life in a positive space,
you open the door for many good things to happen...even love.
And OH, DID IT, and very unexpectedly. It was August 22, 2013, when
my life changed in a way that could only be destined. For as long as I can
remember, I had ONE rule regarding men I would date: Never date a
man you meet in a nightclub. Why? Because most men in the nightclubs
are not there to pursue a future with a woman, they are there to find

a woman or women to "jump off" with. I was never comfortable being that kind of woman.

A male coworker and I made plans a few hours after work to meet at a restaurant for dinner and drinks to celebrate his birthday. I was not able to go right after work because I had scheduled a one-hour boudoir photoshoot. After my photoshoot, I put back on my black pencil dress and red belt, grabbed my red stilettos, and walked out of my hotel room (I was staying the night in the city since I was flying to San Antonio to visit my mother the next day).

Dinner and drinks were good, and after we left the restaurant, we just walked and chatted about work and travel. As we walked, we saw a sign outside a nightclub called Bar 7 that promoted a live go-go band playing. He said he knew the girl who was singing, and so we went in to listen. I got a glass of wine and walked closer to the stage to stand and listen. My coworker tapped me on the shoulder and leaned over, saying to me, "See, you are not the only one who likes Gucci." I looked to my left and saw a brown skin man wearing all white standing in the "Table service" area. As I looked at him, we both smiled, and I motioned for him to come here. He walked to the other side of the VIP booth he was in, leaned over, and then I asked him, "Are those knockoffs?" He looked at me, laughed, and said, "Naw, slim, they aren't knockoffs." We just laughed about it. He said he would offer me a drink, but he didn't want to offend (and he pointed to my coworker). I let him know who he was and that we were not involved, only coworkers. He introduced himself and offered me a drink. I declined and let him know I was only drinking wine, but joined him for a bit. We spent the next few minutes standing and chatting about why he was there. After about 10 minutes, his friend came up and asked Jay to send pictures and any videos of him performing, but there were none. Jay didn't even know his friend performed. Though I was giving Jay every reason not to be interested in me, it felt as if there was no one else in the club but us. Even as I write, I don't remember seeing much of anything other than us in our own world, chatting.

We exchanged numbers before I left. I take that back. I asked him to give me his phone after he asked for my number, and I put my number in and then called myself to have his number. Afterwards, I left for my hotel room to get some sleep before my 6:00 a.m. flight. Before going to bed, I received a text that read, "It was nice to meet you. I hope you made it back to your room safely." I texted back, "Likewise," and went to sleep.

It was about 3 days before we spoke again because I had spent the weekend in Austin, Texas, at Bat Fest with my mom, and both of our phones had died (we had forgotten our chargers). As soon as I got back to San Antonio and plugged my phone up to charge, I had a voicemail from Mr. Bar 7. I returned the call and from there. Our relationship began to evolve.

Naturally Organic

Within the first few months, he and I spent a lot of time together (unless he had his daughter with him). I was in the last few months of my doctoral program, so I had to manage my time around our organically growing relationship (which consisted of hanging out quite a bit). Because of our educational differences, he didn't always understand when I needed to stay in the house and do schoolwork. I was almost finished with my program, and not just writing my dissertation, but also doing classwork.

I feel like it was a whirlwind relationship that went by in slow motion. His security as a man and his high self-esteem made me connect even more with him. Being in a relationship where you don't have to lie about having male friendships was a huge ordeal for me. In turn, he maintained his as well. Believe me, I was the same way with him when it came to my personal security and self-esteem. Perhaps it was merely our maturity and mutual respect for one another that made the difference. We genuinely had a relationship that budded authentically from a friendship. At this time in our relationship, I frequently traveled (which was nearly every month), and not once did he ever complain, nor take issue with it. As a matter of fact, he was never bothered by it at all. In my mind, he was checking all of the boxes for what I sought in a companion.

Within those first few months, we spent a great deal of time together, getting to know one another. We also had some of the most hilarious and embarrassing moments together. He fell down my steps, I fell off my bed and hurt my leg, he ruined our first Valentine's Day together because he had some bad Thai lemon chicken, and so many more hilarious moments. As a matter of fact, at one point, he asked me to never lose the silly part of me. I thought that was just the sweetest thing.

One of the best parts of our relationship was that we had weekly date nights. And they were not always normal date nights either (i.e., bike ride and bar hop around the city, go wine or beer tasting, and once we even did a sip and paint). Another rarity for me was that I got to know many of his friends, who eventually became my friends. Again, he was winning my heart more and more.

Five months passed, and we traveled together for the first time to Las Vegas and Los Angeles. This was the most fun and laughs I had ever had with a man. I am not saying I never had fun with anyone I dated or was previously married to, but this was definitely different. We were both completely okay with being inseparable for days under the same roof. Don't get me wrong, we didn't spend nearly as many nights together early in our relationship. It was "nearly" because when we first met, he lived at his mom's. So, unless we got a hotel room, or he drove up to my house (almost an hour away), we did not spend nights together. But trust me, that did not stop us from connecting often. Or at least as much as I could when I didn't have the responsibility of the school, and he didn't have the responsibility of his daughter (which was another attribute I love about him). As a daddy's girl, there is nothing better than knowing a man loves his daughter and is constantly making sure she is provided for – even when he is not with her. Honestly, it felt so surreal to be with someone like him. A real needle in the haystack! AND THEN...

Seven months into our relationship, I finished my dissertation defense. It was the most exhilarating feeling I've ever experienced. I had spent many weeks in the house writing nonstop, I had cried for days straight, lost six pounds, and didn't really want to talk to anyone other than my mother. Because of her, I was able to persevere. After my defense was over, I called him to tell him the good news. No answer. I called again and got no answer. What the fuck! Not on the most important night of my academic career!! When he finally called back, he explained he was helping his daughter with her homework at his baby momma's house. That, to me, was not a reason to ignore my calls. Did he not know how special a moment this was for me? Guess what? He didn't get it. He really didn't get it. While he wasn't insecure about it, he didn't really understand what I had to go through to attain this. At that moment, it made me look at him differently and feel differently. Not in a bad way, but I had then recognized we value things differently (not that his daughter was not important. I am certainly not saying that). What I am saying is that not answering my call because of where you were was disappointing to me. Was this a deal-breaker or something we could work through? And for a while, I did work through it. Actually, "we" did for another 7 months (by this time, we had been together just over a year).

Although we were close and often told one another we loved each other, he began to act differently. I knew something was wrong, but he would not say. No matter how many times I would ask, he would say he was fine. Until one day, out of the blue, he said he wasn't happy. I admit I was shocked to hear this. Had he been faking how he felt all of this time? I am not the needy type, so it certainly wasn't because I smothered him.

After all, how I lived my life did not change that much. I still traveled with my family and friends, went to happy hour with my friends, had ladies' night, and was happy just being alone. I never complained about the time he spent with me or how much time he spent with friends at the bar, either. So, how the hell can he not be happy? But okay, if that is how you feel, let's take some time apart, and we did. I was confused and heartbroken, but I was completely fine with it.

Walked Away, BUT Was Not Waiting

The next day, I did not send a morning text or call him like I had on any other day. Again, what I refused to do was with someone who does not want to be with me or is unhappy with me. NOT GOING TO HAPPEN! I had been down that road before and knew nothing good would or could come from forcing anything to "be." But then he texted me, "No morning text," with a sad tear-dropping emoji. Why would he think I would text him? If you aren't happy, we won't be friends. I explained to him that I did not...no, no...I could not be friends with him, so I had no reason to text. It was too hard for me emotionally. When I finally decided to answer his call, he explained it was not that he was unhappy but that he was scared. Scared? This was new for me to hear. He then said, "Have you ever prayed for something that seemed impossible to get, and then you get it? You feel like it is too good to be true. I didn't feel like I deserved you." In my mind, all I could think was, "Why was it for him to decide what I deserved"? But if this was his truth, I could not resolve those feelings for him. But if you are scared now, how do I know if that changes if I take you back?

We spent much of 2015 not "together" but in touch, and him having to prove to me that I was what he wanted. I made it very clear that I WAS SINGLE!! I dated other men, traveled to Cabo, Mexico, and Egypt with another man (a friend), and lived my life every bit like I was single. Did it hurt him? From what I was told by him, his friends, and his family...YES. But guess what, I was not bothered if it did or did not. YES, I LOVED HIM, but that love would NEVER weigh more than I loved MYSELF. I was now at the highest level of love I would ever know (sitting on my pedestal)

I turned 40 years old in 2015 and was a very SINGLE woman. My birthday party was what made me change how I felt about him and made me believe him when he said I was what he wanted. He showed and proved he was truly my best friend (through it all). I woke up to my sister and not him, and felt a hurt in my heart I did not expect. He showed me I was what he wanted, but respected me enough not to stay with me while I was passed out drunk (yes, my 40th birthday party was "off the damn chain"). During my party, he also showed me he was willing to be vulnerable. He did not plan to attend my birthday party, but he did just for me. ME! He made sure everything about my party was about me. He looked out for me in a way no other man who was there did. After that day, I knew he realized what he had in me. And I certainly knew what I had in him. He was it (I hoped).

I am a firm believer that normal is subjective. I mean, really, what does that really mean? Relationships are hard! It is work! It has an intentional relationship with another being that is different from you. But when you genuinely love one another, you really begin to understand what it means when the bible says, "Love is patient."

After my birthday, things were perfect. He gave in to his fear of commitment, and every day, I felt loved. He actually got a passport and was open to traveling abroad with me (and we did and had the best time together). I am not saying things were "perfect-perfect" because that would be a stone-cold lie, but what I am saying is that we gave each other a reason to want to stay and make it work every day.

UNTIL...

Growing Pains

After about a year, he began to have guilty feelings from being "too" happy. Feeling guilty that he was putting his happiness over his daughter's, he started to change. Here we go again! If there is one thing I believe in (and actually know), it is that no matter how much you love your children, your happiness matters, too (especially when the love is healthy). I mean, after all, how do you think kids learn what healthy love looks like? And like before, he started acting differently and being distant.

Much like the previous time, and very off guard, he woke me up out of my sleep around 3 am wanting to talk. This was so not like him at all, so it must have weighed heavily on his heart. He indicated he felt guilty for not trying to make things work with his daughter's mother. He admitted he had no feelings at all for her and did not want her, BUT he didn't want to hurt his daughter either. He said he was very confused about what to do. I asked him, "What does that even mean"?

THIS was very new to me and some real shit at that. I have been through a lot and have heard a lot of things, but certainly none at this level. I told him he needed to think about what he wanted, but that if he went back to her, it was OVER!! This was not an ultimatum. This was my reality. You can't go where you have been unhappy and have no feelings and expect it to work. My other reality is that there is no way I will ever be a 2nd choice when I have been nothing but good to him.

The next day, I went home, but we chatted on the phone before I went to brunch with some friends. When I called, he texted that he was in the movies. I said okay, and for him to call me when he got out. Guess what… no call. And I mean no call at all the rest of the day. He went missing in action (aka MIA). I called, but then none of my calls were answered. It got to be really late, and it was unusual not to hear from him, so I got worried. Around 10 or 11 pm, I went to his place only to find he had not been there at all since he left that early afternoon. The lights were still out, but the balcony blinds were still open. Okay, this is definitely not like him. In a panic, I called his mom, his sister, and his grandmother. None of them heard from him. He had an iPad under the table, so I used that to locate his phone, and an address came up. I went to where it said it was last (before it died – his calls were going straight to voicemail). That is when I saw it. His car. Parked where it should not be parked overnight. My heart broke, but I saw red.

I called his phone and cussed him out on his voicemail (letting him know I saw his car). I also went back to his house and packed up EVERY-THING I had recently decorated the apartment with and took it to my house. And I do mean EVERYTHING, including the mirrors on the wall and the bathroom mats!! Yes, I know it was very petty of me. In my anger, I felt no bitch was benefiting from a space I created for his and my comfort. FUCK naw! Not then and not any day! After I put everything in my house, I went back to his house, sat on the couch, and waited for him to show up (which was the next morning). He walked into the house as if I should not have been mad. While he claimed nothing happened, I didn't believe him. Why would he do this to me? He swore he had only taken the kids to the movies and then fell asleep on the couch. Wait, what? His ass was gone all damn day. We need to talk because I certainly did not plan to live like this. He opened up more about his guilt about being young when they tried to make it work, and that while he loved me, he wondered if he owed it to his daughter to try to make things work with her mom since they were more mature and "different" now. OH, REALLY!? REALLY? I could not believe what I was hearing. I was not mad, but I was very hurt to hear all of this. Who wouldn't be? SO, how long has this conversation been going on between them behind my back? I felt a lot of things, but more than anything, I went numb. Then I left. My heart died that day, and so did everything I felt about us being together.

I Choose ME

The next day, he had his daughter, yet he was blowing up my phone. I was absolutely in a place unfamiliar to me and ignored every single call. It was as if I was not able to breathe. When I finally answered the phone that evening, I had a meltdown and unleashed everything I had ever felt (including how betrayed I felt). You see, one thing I was NOT going to be was what I did not deserve to be...SECOND! I told him I was way too good to him to have to compete with ANY WOMAN. He apologized profusely and told me he loved me and that I was what he wanted. That was not enough. When it comes to my heart, I will always choose me over someone else choosing me second. I was never going to settle for less than what I deserved, and I would rather love and let go than not be treated the way I treated him...RESPECTFULLY. I had been more than patient and beyond understanding of the ignorance, jealousy, and immaturity I had to tolerate from a woman I had never met and who had never met me.

He wanted to make it work with me. I don't care how uncharted the waters are; LOVE is love, and you pour into it (especially when it is healthy), not be scared of it. I needed time to think it over because I could not let him keep running in and out of my life. My emotions were exposed, but my senses were intact!

Chapter Five

Trust In Fate

"If you truly value something, let it go with trust. If it returns, it was always meant for you. If not, honor its path, release it with gratitude, and know that what's meant for you will always find its way." – Dr. P. Gurley

When you operate from a healed place, you become cognizant that your emotional awareness is heightened. You also don't choose to run from them, and instead face them head-on. Your sense is your intuition speaking to you. At least that was how it was (and is) for me. That is why I needed time. I had to stand still and listen to what my body was telling me, not just my heart. I didn't have room in my life to live through another emotional heartbreak. Being scared to love is one thing, but choosing *not* to be happy is a whole other level of a curveball I never saw coming.

Let me tell you something: Being healed allows you to see the human in people. (especially the one(s) you love). It allows you to understand that everyone's personal growth does not run parallel (especially in relationships). And it often occurs when hurt, pain, or other life experiences trigger what can be a life-altering decision. Who was I to say what he was feeling was wrong to feel (especially when it had never been experienced)? I didn't have to like it, but I did have to respect the honesty for the space he was in.

So, instead of being open to taking him back immediately, I gave him space. I needed him to work through his emotions regarding his daughter and his own happiness. I was not at all sure what that would take, but I also know I needed time to work through my own emotions surrounding our relationship. It was important to me that we would not end up here again, and there was no rushing when it came to love. I also refused to lie to myself about the stakes of his decision. That would be too much like reverting back to who I used to be, and I refused to become her again.

Hell, I know I could never be her again anyhow. My internal growth didn't bury her; it matured her.

When you have a relationship built on organic friendship, communication rarely stops because there is "space" between two people. And perhaps it was only like that for us, but I do know I had never experienced what was transpiring between us. He wanted what he wanted and never stopped pursuing me. In that, he showed up intentionally. What he did differently was choose to become more open about his past [traumas]. Things I am certain never had a reason to surface until he fell in love with me and added what felt like was confusion or conflicting to his co-parenting. It's remarkable how someone's childhood can significantly impact their future. I mean, I know this happens, I guess I just never saw it happening when a relationship is pretty much perfect. But then, isn't that how life works? When things seem perfect, there are always lessons of growth to bring discomfort. That is where trusting in fate comes in. And that trust has more to do with us within than the other person.

Trust is organic. You either have it or you don't. Trust is also internal. It is the most intangible quality we have, and we give. It forms the foundation for every meaningful connection we build. Unlike skills or credentials, trust cannot be forced, taught, or externally imposed. It must be nurtured from within. When it is absent or broken, even the strongest relationships can unravel. Ultimately, trust is a reflection of our values and intentions, quietly shaping how we show up for ourselves and for others every day. And he and I chose to show up not just for ourselves but also for our relationship.

After a few weeks of talking, we decided to make it work. I made it very clear that if we were ever back in this space at all, there would be no reconciliation, no understanding, no patience, and no friendship. Yes, I was willing to "dead" it all. I was going to choose myself and honor the closing of this path and be open-hearted to whatever would have come.

Looking back, it's easy to romanticize the moments that led us here. To recall the laughter on long road trips to my mom's, the exuberant amount of laughs traveling together or with friends, the quiet comfort of shared silence over dinner or while watching television, or the late-night bar conversations that stitched our hearts closer together. But the truth is, our journey was never about perfection; it was about persistence, patience, and the courage to trust in something bigger than ourselves. Fate, in its mysterious wisdom, brought us back to each other (or rather, kept us together) not because we were flawless, but because we were willing to do the work, to grow, and to choose each other every single day.

It's said that love is not just a feeling, but a series of choices. I learned this in the spaces between our pain and our forgiveness. We chose to listen, even when it was hard. We chose kindness over ego, compassion over pride. We chose to see the best in each other, especially in the moments when our worst selves threatened to take center stage. Trusting in fate didn't mean waiting passively for happiness to arrive; it meant actively participating in our own healing, and in the healing of our relationship. There were times when the future felt uncertain, when the weight of our past threatened to overshadow the possibility of joy. But with every challenge, we built something stronger. A friendship that refused to fade, a partnership rooted in mutual respect, and a love that could withstand the storms. We learned that it's not about avoiding pain, but about learning how to hold it together, to support one another through the messiness of life.

Over the years, we became each other's safe haven. We traveled to new places, not just to escape, but to discover the world together, making memories one city, one adventure, one memory at a time. Each journey became another thread in the tapestry of our story, a reminder that growth is ongoing and that love, when nurtured, only deepens with time.

We supported each other through career transitions, business ventures, and personal reinventions. There were seasons of abundance and seasons of loss, but through it all, we never lost sight of the friendship that was the foundation of our relationship. When one of us stumbled, the other extended a hand. When doubts crept in, we reminded each other of our shared dreams and the promises we made, not just as lovers, but as best friends.

Kindness became our currency. We learned to apologize without reservation, to forgive without keeping score, and to celebrate each other's wins as if they were our own. Our relationship is not defined by grand gestures or social media highlights, but by the quiet moments of care. From bringing me kombucha in the morning, to how I listen when he needs to vent after a long day. These small acts, repeated over the years, have become the bedrock of our life together.

On February 24, 2024, after 10 and a half years of growing, learning, and loving, we stood before our closest friends and family and said, "I do." It wasn't just a wedding; it was a celebration of everything we had endured and everything we had become together. It was a testament to the power of patience, the necessity of forgiveness, and the beauty of trusting in fate. And while my wedding did not go as planned (which I had to come to grips with after all of the money it cost), I know what matters most is what happens afterwards.

After 12 years together, we have a marriage grounded in friendship, kindness, and unwavering support. If there is one lesson I hope you take from our story, it's this: Trust in fate, but also trust in yourself. Trust that you are worthy of love that is gentle and true. Trust that even when the path is unclear, the universe has a way of bringing you exactly where you are meant to be. And when you find someone who meets you with honesty, with care, and with the willingness to build something lasting, hold on, nurture it, and let it grow. Our journey was never linear, and it was never easy. But it was real. And in the end, that's what matters most. We are living proof that love, when built on friendship and trust, can weather any storm and blossom into something extraordinary.

So, here's to the pain that shaped us, the fate that reunited us, and the friendship that sustains us. Here's to trusting in the journey, and to believing that the best is always yet to come.

I found my forever, y'all!

Part 2 My Thoughts

Chapter Six

Imposter Syndrome

"We live in societies that, if we are not true to ourselves, someone else will determine the truth for us, and that sucks! How sad it must be to wake up every day knowing that you are not at peace with who you are. You become an imposter in your own life." - Malebo Sephodi (2015)

B eing a double minority, I have always been very cognizant of the fact that I was going to have to work harder than most women. What I was not cognizant of was how I would feel once I began to collect milestones of success. Every bit of my existence as an adult was to pursue things I love and am passionate about, even if the benefit was indirect (i.e., mentoring or coaching someone else into their greatness). I am admittedly an obsessive overachiever, but I also admit that I spent the majority of my existence "in the dark" because I questioned my abilities. I wish I knew the turning point in my life where I began to fall victim to imposter syndrome. Wait, let me back up five seconds. Let me be honest and say what I know you all are thinking: "What the fuck is imposter syndrome?" Like you, I was not even aware there was such a thing. It became a title to what I was battling, so let me not sit here and pretend to be an expert on the subject. I just know that it is something I suffered from (God, bless literature and books on the subject). Okay, let me rewind that one more time. It is probably inaccurate to say that this is past tense for me. I find myself having to mentally check myself more often than not when it comes to this.

As I was stating, I wish I knew where this mindset turned. When I was a preteen and a teen, I was a gifted poet, writer, and editor. I know this may be hard to believe since it is rarely (if ever) mentioned, but this is very true. I say gifted because poetry manifested in my sleep, and I'd wake and write an entire poem (sometimes gospel music) in its entirety. No, I am not one of those people who can recall anything that I have ever written, like many "spoken word" poets (and yes, that level of talent makes me a bit envious), but I can write with an ease that comes naturally and methodically, as if someone took over my body to compose beautiful pieces of work. By the way, while I have two poems published in compilation books, this is not something many people know (or know) about me. I have a few written (literally) books in my home that are on my bookshelf, filled with unshared poetry I have no intent on sharing with the world. I consider it my private collection. Don't ask me why that is. Perhaps this is another area of my imposter syndrome, of feeling it is not good enough.

My earliest (and fondest) memory of exerting a level of editorial professionalism is when my mom trusted me to proofread her dissertation while I was in 9th grade. Yes, you read that right, I was in 9th grade proofing a master's thesis! Pivotal reflections like that with my mom shaped me in understanding I was gifted and different. She was/is as intelligent as she was/is street smart (she was born and bred in Washington, DC, and no matter how many years pass in age, that street sense shit just never leaves). Since my dad was in the military, she chose to ensure my sisters and I were not raised in the same environment (though we spent every summer and Spring break in Washington, and she taught us to be as street smart as we were book smart). Anyhow, my mom has never not supported me or my sisters and has a knack for just knowing our strengths and pouring into those things. I mean, seriously, the energy she gave us was never ceasing. My older sister and I were in the Upward Bound program, where we went to college while in high school. During my time in the program, I was also the Editor-in-Chief of the magazine for the program, so trust me, my editorial skills have been around for a long time. This is probably the only area I feel confident in.

Now, how on earth do I go from a level of non-degree educated and filled with confidence to doctoral educated and feeling like an imposter to my own knowledge, skills, and abilities? This is what I found baffling. How does that happen? I have watched white women stand confidently in their education and abilities (titles and all) and let the world know "HERE I AM, HERE I STAND." Part of me felt that level of confidence is not always met with the same level of perception if delivered by me. You see, melanin women are seen as angry when we are assertive. Or we think "we know it all" or are "better than" others when we flex that same level of confidence, but I digress because that is a chapter of its own. But you know what happens when you do not own your assertiveness? It is equally as demeaning and a mental blow to our professional and personal self-worth.

In 2013, I accepted a budget formulation analyst position at a Federal agency. It was an interesting transition because the timing could not have come at a worse time in my life. I had just moved into a brand-new house 64 miles away, just 9 months earlier, and was in the last year of my Doctoral program (which is the most crucial year). Anyhow, within the first few weeks I was there, a colleague stopped by my cubicle to make small talk. It was a Friday, so he asked if I had weekend plans. I politely let him know that I had no plans, as I had reading to do and a paper to write for school. He said, "Oh, so you are in school?" and then he asked, "For what?" Before I could respond, he followed up with, "So you are getting your Bachelor's?" I indicated I was not, and he cut me off before I could continue with my answer and said, "Oh, so you are getting your Master's?" I again indicated I was not and proceeded to say I was attaining my Doctorate, but was cut off yet again. This time, I was hit with the ultimate insult. He said, "Oh, so you are getting a certificate?" I admit I was immediately taken aback. Is this what he really thinks, because I am dripping in golden melanin and look younger than I am? What on earth would make him think I would not be capable of succeeding at that level of academia (especially to reduce the level of education opportunity to a certificate)? It is quite insulting that someone would go from a master's to a certificate as opposed to saying, "Oh, so you're getting a doctorate." Even when I did indicate I was getting my doctorate, he looked at me in a condescending way and said, "Oh, that's impressive." It is already bad enough that other races don't find black women capable of academic or professional success at higher-than-average levels, and it is more demeaning when our "brothers" insinuate the same.

Fast forward a few years, and not once but twice, I have been pulled into an office to have a discussion over my email signature consisting of my title being "Dr. Pamela Gurley, D.M." Two different agencies, two different sexes, and guess what...both bursting with melanin. Even worse, both times, there was always some hesitation or discomfort while bringing it up. What was odder was that they both basically stated close to the same thing: "I recognize your signature is very formal. Here we are very informal, and you don't want to come across the wrong way. There are lots of PhDs here, and none of them put that in their signature. I know you worked hard, and you don't have to change it, but I just want you to know how it looks." While I never thought to change it, I wondered "who" was looking at it and feeling some kind of way. Or is it uncomfortable for someone who does not have it? Don't get me wrong,

I have never been the type of person to wear my education or titles on my sleeve, nor do I demand to be called Dr. Gurley. I actually prefer to keep all my relationships informal (though I would never go by Miss, Ms., or Mrs. [when I remarry] because I did earn the title through my hard work, sacrificed time, and lots of tears). So, here is a bigger secret I have never openly shared: I never desired to be called Dr. Gurley because I didn't want anyone to judge me. Or perhaps I judged myself and was afraid, "I," thought I was not worthy of such a title. What a way to devalue my hard work and money spent (because, let's face it, education is hella expensive). But at some point, you have no choice but to face reality and realize that if you demean yourself, it leaves room for others to do the same thing. So, I had to change the way I thought.

It's extremely frustrating to hear you intimidate people all the time. I, myself, cannot possibly intimidate people; people allow themselves to be intimidated by me or intimidated by anyone that they find intimidating. Understand this: I have been purposeful in the decisions that I made in my life (good, bad, or indifferent). I have been purposeful in the things that I wanted to achieve, and I achieved those things. I can't speak on someone else's decision to be driven or not.

Here is what I will say about perceptions: when you run into people of "likeness," you are inevitably going to stand out (and not in the sense that you are probably thinking). By "stand out," I mean someone who moves like you, is ambitious like you, or sees great things in you, will take notice of YOU!! You cannot hide. Your knowledge, skills, talents, energy…you name it, it draws them! This is how I was pulled out of the shadows and into "the light."

Against everything I believed about myself being in the public eye, I finally decided to be open to sharing who I was when I was nominated to be one of "the top 100 women you need to know" by a nonprofit organization called Saving Her Elegance. Before then, I kind of liked… no, no, no, I preferred to be in the shadows. I liked not being out there, subjecting myself to criticism or judgment. I don't necessarily know why I internalized it and why I would be bothered by the words of others; however, if I am honest with myself, it was often based on my experience with walking into places and people's first perception of me. This time, the opportunity was different. It was as though I met the person who forced me to really step full throttle into my purpose…Natasha Lee.

Natasha and I met ONCE at a bridal shower in Detroit and instantly connected. Her energy, her vibrant no-nonsense attitude, and she will succeed no matter who she has to "check." She was the "HERE I AM. HERE I STAND" woman, but she took it further. She had the "I AM THAT GIRL" attitude!! She inspired me to see myself differently and pushed me to limits I did not think were possible "out in the open" for everyone to see. She made me accountable for how I should see myself and trust myself. Everything with her was, "Pam, you can do it. You got this!"

And guess what? I did have it and I got it...over and over and over again!

I have always known you had to be ambitious about what you want and go after it and make sacrifices in order to achieve it. In other words, you have to be intentional and purposeful. When you walk in your purpose and you "make it," you shouldn't feel bad for it. When I used to hear people tell me, "You intimidate people," that's what felt...somewhat bad for all I had accomplished. I was also hearing being told I need to dumb myself down, so I don't make other people feel uncomfortable. That's not a burden of feelings for me to carry. That's actually nobody's burden to carry, AND you are outright asking people not to be happy for the things that they have been purposeful in accomplishing. Being purposeful is living in your truth, and I'm always going to live in my truth, and if it hurts other people, that's not my problem. This is why I am proud of myself for not changing my signature to make other people comfortable. The other thing I am most proud of is that it never changed the perception of who I was within my personal and professional relationships, nor how deeply they were forged.

Chapter Seven

Natural Discomfort

I cried, I cried... it was such an emotional experience, and it wasn't just about hair. It was what my perception of beauty was and had been for all of my life, and then I look at myself in the mirror, and I'm like, 'That doesn't look like what I thought was beautiful.'" -Teyonah Parris

I am not sure what it is, but I have nearly always had a love-hate relationship with my hair. I loved it when it was relaxed (which was only two to three times a year after I turned 16 or 17 years old), and at times, I hated how fast it grew in between because it was hard to wrap and go. It was not until I was in my 40s that I decided to go natural. I take that back, I tried once in my 20s, and I lasted less than a month and said to myself, "hell no, this ain't gonna work!" Shortly after that decision, I let it grow out many times but would cut it shoulder or chin length until I decided to stop cutting it altogether after I cut it off all the way to my ears (and oh, did it grow). Over the course of five years, my hair grew from by my ears to down to the middle of my back, and I loved it! The only problem was that it came with more criticism than I expected.

"Long Hair, Don't Care"

Having long, relaxed hair, I never thought so many people would have so much to say. After all, most people get weaves and wigs to have straight hair down their backs, to their shoulders, or over their boobs. But nope, I was almost always asked, "Where do you buy your hair from?" "Is that all your hair?" and the one I hated the most was, "It's so pretty; can I feel it?" Here's a HUGE stereotype breaker: melanin women can have long hair, and it's not fake. Now, let me be more direct. Melanin women, we can have long hair, so please stop criticizing those who do.

In 2007 (maybe 2008), I was attending a comedy show by a really good comedian friend of mine named Red Bone (he was also performing stand-up that night). It is nothing new for him to "call me out" or call me up on the stage during his set to do something crazy like throw dollar bills at me. Quite honestly, any chance he got to be a smart ass when it came to me, he would most certainly make an opportunity of it (even to this day). At this particular show, when he called me up on stage, I made a point to move my hair out of my face once or twice (my hair at that time was a little more than breast length in the front, so it was constantly in my face). Because of the stage lighting, I could not directly see the whole face of the woman at one of the closer tables. Still, I could certainly hear the comments regarding my "swinging" hair and my skin tone (basically stating I thought I was "all of that" because of these two factors). Because I chose to have long hair, it was as though I was persecuted for it. It certainly did not make me feel any kind of way about it. I LOVED my long hair. My hair was a huge part of who I was, and being without it was just not going to happen. Or so I thought.

From 2012 to 2018, I cut my hair and let it grow, cut my hair, and let it grow, and cut my hair and let it grow. It was never really short, but more of a shoulder-length bob. It was easy, convenient, and most of all, it could go up into a ponytail whenever I wanted (this was hella important for me). I had pretty much always done my own hair, and it was tamed, so it was extremely easy to manage. I also attribute it to my hair being relaxed and being most often wrapped at night and taken down in the morning. Yes, ba-bae, my hair was super tamed from this! Even after I stopped relaxing it in March 2017, my wash and blow were tamed and manageable. The need to no longer relax my hair became stronger and stronger, as did my need to start trimming my hair regularly to start the natural hair transition. And then, on May 26, 2018, I decided to do the ultimate...the BIG CHOP!!!

Emotionally Traumatized

If you really want to experience self-hatred and an extreme amount of insecurity, cut all of your hair off. I swear the big chop will literally wipe most or every bit of self-esteem away that you have. At least it was certainly the case for me. It was hard for me to look at myself and be happy. It was just so...short! It was then that I realized how much mental stock I put into my hair and what it meant when it came to beauty. It defined who I was. It made me feel like a woman. I no longer felt like I was as beautiful as I was with my long or shoulder-length, straight hair. I spent weeks at a time researching hair types just to get a better understanding of products said to be good for naturally curly hair or "good hair." I mean, really, what does that even mean? And for the life of me, why is there a need to texture type black hair? Variations of curly, variations of kinky, 2A, 3C, 4B...I mean, really, why can't black women just have beautiful hair? To add insult to injury, I had no fucking idea what to do with my hair after making this newfound decision. I probably should have done more research on the emotional transition, not the physical, before taking such a leap. After all, hair is not something you can just hide. It is very present-day in and day out. It just sits there...out in the open, looking good or looking bad. Well, I guess I could have gotten a wig, worn a scarf, or had some hair sewn in, but that is just not my thing. I have only had sewn-ins twice while on vacation, and it came out of my head as soon as I got home - both times.

No number of compliments made me feel better or good about myself. I was the person having to live with this look and find some level of peace with it. It did not come easy. I loved my texture; I just had no idea how to do anything with it. It was difficult taking selfies or being in pictures because I didn't feel beautiful. I felt pretty at times, but never beautiful. A month after my big chop, I thought about getting micro braids, and I knew for sure it would make me feel better about myself. Just as fast as I thought it, I just as quickly acknowledged how unhealthy my thoughts were about how I felt about myself and this new look. I made the decision to spend most of my summer heat-free and braid-free so I could learn to embrace this new normal. It was probably the most liberating decision I had ever made, and I came to love myself so much that I cut it short again about five months later (though not as short, but short enough).

Anti-social Reality

Though natural hair is pretty common for black women to have now, it is not as widely accepted in every social setting. I work and play in Washington, DC.; therefore, I am never short of being around people in professional or social settings. When my hair is blown straight, many more people speak to me or ask me for directions, are more friendly, or just strike up casual conversations. When my hair is curly, I don't get the same level of interaction. By no means am I indicating people are unfriendly or disrespectful; they are just different and distant in their actions. It is as though they are more comfortable and are more relatable with someone who looks more "like them." And you know what...that is okay. What is not okay is to stereotype, thinking that women with natural hairstyles are any different from women with straight hair. WE ARE NOT! We speak the same, drink the same, eat the same...do everything the same. I, myself, wear my hair more naturally now to ensure the narrative changes. Let's face it, it is the only way for more people to be exposed to it.

Representation matters. It was great having more celebrities choose to represent natural hairstyles because little girls need that. I wish I had more representation of it when I was younger. Well, there was Grace Jones, who certainly represented everything beautiful, dark, and natural. I remember how strong she was and unapologetic about how she looked. She was so fierce. It has been a few years since I have seen anything about her, but I would imagine she is still everything she was before. There was also Thelma from Good Times, but let's be honest, other than a few, they never showed how many exciting things could be done with natural hair. Trust me, I can understand why; though I am happy to see so many beautiful things women are doing with their natural hair, this is not the case for me.

As my hair has grown, I learned to embrace it. I still have no idea what to do with it, but I can pull it up into a ponytail, and I have finally tamed a part to stay. I have also found products I love to use that work for me (I cannot even begin to explain the hundreds of dollars I have spent trying to find something that works). I have watched videos, read articles, and followed natural hair social media accounts to help me in my transition. It has been a year, and guess what, I still have no fucking idea how to do a lot with my hair. I get by, but I am certainly not creative, nor do I have many styles. But you know what, I am quite okay with that!

Quick Update: While I did not want to rewrite any part of this chapter, I do want to update that I did learn to not only manage my natural hair; I learned to style it. I fell in love with it at every stage of growth. I had never before [as an adult] seen my natural hair long. I grew it waist length, dyed it blond, and just had a lot of fun with it. Rarely did I wear protective styles because I loved my natural curls that much. Wash and go was literally my jam. And as I approach 50, I slowly began to cut it and recently (Oct 2025) did another big chop. This time, there was no emotional trauma or discomfort; only loving the hair God gave me. It is beautiful both long and short.

Chapter Eight

Why Is It So Damn Hot?

"Growing up, I thought the biggest secret was how to deal with periods. Turns out, the real mystery is why my internal thermostat now thinks I live on the equator." – Dr. P. Gurley

I f someone had told my teenage self that the hottest part of womanhood wouldn't be summer time in a bikini at the beach sipping drinks, but a heatwave that strikes at random, I would have laughed. Yet here I am, approaching my 50th birthday, easily hot and sometimes sweating in some of the most random places, wondering why no one ever warned me about this stage of life. This was never a lesson in sexual education courses when they talked about the body maturing. Or maybe I was absent that day. But I would have loved to know what was beyond the mental period.

The mystery is that not only does it happen to every woman at varying ages, but perimenopause and menopause also look very different for every woman. For me, I had early onset perimenopause because I had a partial hysterectomy at 38 (got rid of it all except my ovaries). I know that seems pretty young (especially since I did not have any children). But I had fibroids, and I only had it in me to have surgery once and once only. In my research, they were known to come back, and I personally knew women who had several fibroid surgeries because they wanted to have children. Well, I was not one of those women. I didn't want or desire to have children (at least not biologically). I have always been extremely maternal; I just liked kids better when I could give them back and go about my life. The funny (or maybe not so funny) actuality was that I was scheduled for fibroid removal surgery, and when I went for my pre-op, I changed my mind to having a hysterectomy (again, because I had taken the time to do a lot of research). My doctor (who was very pregnant at the time) asked me if I was sure and stated, "This is final." I assured her of my decision and why—I also had Adenomyosis (which is something else there is not enough discussion about, but I digress).

I want to say I transitioned into perimenopause around seven years or so after my hysterectomy. While I was used to occasionally having night sweats from when I did have a period, what was new were the hot and then not hot moments. Neither peri- nor menopause comes with a universal set of instructions or even a reliable schedule. The heat would sneak up like a thief in the middle of the night. One moment I'd be sleeping peacefully, and the next I'd be kicking off covers, desperate to cool off and looking for cool spots within the sheets, only to get cold just as quickly and pull the covers back on me. Oh, and let's talk about the "water shows" your body decides it wants to perform. Sweat would show up in the most unexpected places—my neck, behind my knees, my stomach, the bends of my elbows—like my body had its own secret performance schedule, but like an unsynchronized sprinkler system since it did not happen in those places all at once. The unpredictability was half the challenge: sometimes it was a gentle warmth, other times a full-blown inferno. And while I'd always heard a few laughable conversations about hot flashes, I never realized just how disruptive and oddly specific they could be until I was living through them.

When I could not go back to sleep, I would conduct late-night internet searches looking for ways to manage what was becoming more and more my new normal. I experimented with home remedies, tried various supplements, and even scheduled appointments with a menopause clinic. All I know is what I was not willing to do, and that was to do any kind of Hormone Replacement Therapy (HRT). Cancer runs in my family, and I didn't want to take any risks. Yes, that makes it harder to manage; however, I do believe there has to be something to provide some level of relief.

What has truly made a difference in how I manage my emotions around it is talking openly with my friends. Our experiences couldn't have been more different. Some started early, others much later, and the symptoms varied wildly. Even with all the advice and products circulating on social media, most of it has felt disconnected from what I was and am actually living. These conversations with my friends remind me that menopause is deeply individual, and that sharing our real stories matters more than any generic solution.

So, maybe the real question isn't "Why is it so damn hot?" but "Why did we wait so long to talk about it?" I may not have all the answers, and my journey is still unfolding. But I know this: I am not alone, and neither are you. Every hot flash, every sleepless night, every unexpected change is just one more chapter in the story of becoming HER. Whole, empowered, and real.

Chapter Nine

Resilience in Real Time

"True resilience is not about how quickly you bounce back,

but how deeply you allow yourself to grow through what

you endure." - Dr. P. Gurley

Resilience is a word that gets thrown around so often that it can start to sound like a cliché. For me, resilience isn't a hashtag or a motivational slogan; it's a living, breathing force that has carried me through the most uncertain seasons of my life. Since 2019, the world has shifted in ways none of us could have predicted. The ground beneath us has moved—sometimes gently, sometimes like an earthquake (honest, all 2025, it has moved like a 15.9 earthquake). Through it all, I have learned that resilience is not something you find in a moment of crisis or want reactively in a moment of crisis. It is something you build, day by day, in real time.

When I reflect on the years since the first edition of this book, I see a series of unexpected challenges: a global pandemic that upended routines and relationships (and also stopped my very first book tour from happening), the ongoing reckoning with racial injustice in America, personal losses, career pivots (I resigned from my Federal position to be a full-time business owner), and the relentless demand to keep showing up. There were days when the weight of uncertainty felt like too much to bear. There were moments when I questioned my own strength and wondered if I had what it took to keep moving forward.

Here's what I know now: resilience is not about never falling apart. It is about allowing yourself to break, to feel, to grieve, and then, slowly, to gather the pieces and build something new. It is about extending the same grace to yourself that you extend to others. In real time, resilience looks like choosing to get out of bed when you'd rather lie there existing instead of living. It's sending that difficult email, setting that boundary, or asking for help when pride tells you to stay silent. It's forgiving yourself for not having all the answers, and trusting that you will find your way, one small step at a time.

I remember a specific day in 2020 when everything felt like it was unraveling. Where I worked was severely toxic, many of my creative projects were stalled, and the world outside my door seemed to be shifting in ways none of us could predict. Yet, the reality is that I made it through the pandemic by choosing to live my life—just at home, in new and meaningful ways.

Instead of retreating into isolation, I found new ways to foster connection and joy. I started a daily "Coffee with Coworkers" Zoom meeting that ran for four hours Monday through Friday, creating a virtual space where colleagues and friends who might otherwise be alone could log in, work alongside each other, and share a laugh or a break together. It became a lifeline for many, a reminder that even in uncertain times, community is possible.

I cooked more than ever before, experimenting with new recipes and growing my own herbs and vegetables in a garden I cultivated with my own hands. Our back patio became a sanctuary, a place where we could gather safely with single friends who might have otherwise felt isolated. Many nights, we ate and drank, sharing stories while listening to music. We created moments of celebration and togetherness, even as the world pressed pause. And when the world opened just a little after a few months, we spent a lot of time in outdoor places.

Resilience, I realized, is not always about pushing through pain or hardship in solitude. Sometimes, it's about creating joy, building community, and finding fulfillment in the present moment—no matter how limited our circumstances may seem. I learned that adapting to new realities can mean discovering new passions, nurturing relationships, and making the ordinary feel extraordinary.

Resilience in real time means adapting to change, even when it's uncomfortable. It means letting go of the version of yourself you thought you had to be and making space for the person you are becoming. It's about learning to pivot when plans fall apart and finding new ways to connect, create, and contribute. For me, that meant embracing virtual speaking engagements, stepping into a new media writing role (first year I did a virtual press call for the Stellar Awards), launching new projects from my home office, taking risks by embracing full-time entrepreneurship, and finding creative ways to stay connected to my community.

One of the most important lessons I've learned is that resilience is not a solo act. It is built in relationship with ourselves, our loved ones, and the communities that hold us up. In the hardest moments, I leaned on my friends, my family, and my faith. I learned to ask for support, to admit when I was struggling, and to receive help with gratitude. I discovered that vulnerability is not a weakness but a source of strength, a bridge that connects us to others in our most human moments.

I've also learned to honor my boundaries. Saying "no" is an act of resilience. Protecting my time and energy is not selfish; it is necessary. I no longer feel guilty for stepping back, for resting, or for prioritizing my own well-being. Resilience means knowing when to push forward and when to pause. It means trusting that rest is not the enemy of progress, but a vital part of the journey.

If you are reading this and wondering how to become more resilient, I want you to know that you already are. Every time you've survived a hard day, every time you've chosen hope over despair, every time you've shown up for yourself or someone else, you have demonstrated resilience. It's not about perfection. It's about persistence, patience, and a willingness to begin again. Resilience in real time is messy. It is nonlinear. Some days you feel strong and unstoppable; other days you feel fragile and uncertain. Both are true. Both are necessary. The key is to keep moving, to keep believing in your own capacity to heal, to grow, and to thrive.

As I write this, I am still learning, still stretching, still becoming. I am grateful for every challenge that has shaped me, for every lesson that has taught me to trust myself a little more. I am grateful for the community of women who remind me that I am never alone in my struggles. Together, we are building a new definition of resilience, one that honors our humanity, our vulnerability, and our power.

So, here's my invitation to you: Give yourself grace on the hard days, and remember that resilience is not about never breaking. It is about choosing, over and over, to put yourself back together, to reach for joy, and to trust that you are enough, just as you are, right now, in real time.

Part 3 My Perspective

Chapter Ten

I Am Not Angry

The only anger I see is from a social society that provokes and judges because we {Black women} have proven to be stronger and more resilient than any other race." - Dr. P. Gurley

I have never really understood the "angry black woman" stereotype. And while I am sure there are some who are, I assure you at least 85-90% of us are not. No black woman is born angry. Quite frankly, women (of any race or ethnicity) are born to nurture. But let's keep it real: Black women only appear angry to a society that has made it a point to break them. A culture that constantly criticizes her. A world that declassifies her. A community that stereotypes her. No one can say it is a lie because there is evidence at every corner of social media, in the newspaper, in magazines, and/or on television. Look at the way society tried to provoke the Former First Lady. Here you have a bold, educated, classy, well-spoken black woman who, at every turn, was criticized for her clothes & demeaned by her looks. And kudos to her for keeping it classy for 8 years and beyond in the public eye.

I also need the critics to understand that it is not that we are angry; it is more so that we are misunderstood because of how we grow from our experiences, share our passions, and set boundaries. You see, we don't have to raise our voices to be considered "angry." If we carry ourselves assertively and/or speak boldly, we are considered "angry." We can have an opinion that does not agree with someone else's and merely stress our point to agree to disagree and be quickly labeled "angry." We cannot want "unwanted" attention and indicate our dislike as a means to have it discontinued and further prevented, and be labeled as angry. It honestly is not a fair judgment or assessment.

Let me let you in on a not-so-secret: I, like any other ethnicity of women (or men), have a right to be angry (especially when warranted). Why? Because it is natural. Because it is an emotion. Because it is a feeling.

BECAUSE it is human. I don't quite understand why it is wrong for a black woman to show anger. Do we turn into a dragon, breathe fire, and burn down a village? In anger, does every black woman commit heinous crimes? I can assure you we do not. We are not that crazy! As a matter of fact, we hurt, we cry, we are silent in pain, and we suffer, no matter how angry or hurt we become. There are so many things in life that can break you, discourage you, and/or fail you. And you know what, how you get up and face each day, will determine your state of mind and your way through things.

I have had my own personal moments in hell, and I am living proof that toxic thoughts and toxic living have a way of bringing out a strength that would make any woman overcome the need for anger. I am not saying I never get angry; I am saying I know how to handle people who think I am. Believe me, I did not get to where I am because I did not know or understand "time and place." I also did not get to where I am because I did not know how to handle disrespect with some form of polite diplomacy while making my point clear. Even in all of that, I was and am always conscientious that I will always be a target for being an "angry black woman."

You see, "we" are not allowed to show weakness. "We" are not allowed to show strength. "We" are not allowed to show professional or personal assertive aggressiveness. There is no happy medium for "us," and it is JUST NOT FAIR!!! As I previously stated, women are born to nurture, not be angry. But Black women were bred to endure suffrage. It is generational. So, no, our display of anger is rarely in public. It is rarely in the face of those who hate us. It is rare because black women have always been slow to anger. Oh, hell yes, "we" can get mad easily (no doubt that), but anger... is a whole other emotion that many can never tap into. Anger is a "passionate" place of hurt for us. It is not easily given and not easily pacified. This is why the stereotype bothers me so much.

I know you wonder what the hell that means, right? Well, if you are wondering that, clearly, you are on the outside desiring to look in... sooooo, let me enlighten you. There are only a few things that anger black women. Suppose you mess with our kids, our money, and our hearts. Every now and again, it can extend to our immediate siblings and family (like me...I am extremely passionate about my nieces and nephews to the point I am willing to go to jail for all of them (security clearance and all)). Oh, and my sisters, too.

Because of this, I also feel as though I am in a position to protect those who lack the will for controversy. I know that sounds strange, but neither of my sisters has ever been a controversial woman. I have been a protector for a very long time. I cannot explain the reasoning for this; however, I will do my best to explain so you (the reader) can understand what it means to be passionate to the point of protecting.

There are very few reasons to get angry (at least for me). I am a "matters of the heart" type of person. Matters of the heart mean that if you are not my mom, sisters, nieces, nephews, or someone I am fucking, I can care less about how you think, what you say, or how you feel. If you mean harm, you will be met with a level of hatred you never knew was possible to walk the earth. Yes, I openly admit, and I HAPPILY own the part of me that would make a person wish they were dead rather than deal with me. This is also how I know I am not easily angered. My thoughts are naturally creative. My thoughts are naturally methodical. When it comes to family, I am passionate. When it comes to everything else, I care a bit less. Reread what I wrote to digest it. "I care a BIT LESS" when it comes to anything and everything outside of my immediate family. Believe me, that is the thought and feelings of most black women associated with the "angry black woman" stereotype. By no means am I saying or implying that I, or black women in general, don't have ill or hurtful feelings when it comes to a man, but we equate that differently than we do our family. I also want to note I did not use the term angry but hurt. I honestly feel men often confuse the two.

There should be no sin in speaking out as a black woman. There should be no punishment for venting and letting out opinions, especially when it is against injustice. We deserve to speak out, and we also deserve to be heard. The black woman is not angry; she just needs to be heard. She needs society to know she matters. She needs the people to know she has a voice. She needs the world to understand she deserves justice and fairness. She only wants a safer and more secure society and a less judgmental and more accepting community. She wants to walk freely without fear of harassment or abuse. She wants equal opportunities for herself and the generation of other young women coming behind her because she owes them that. And nothing should really stand in the way of that. The black woman wants to know that her concerns are genuine and that she's not insane for having a voice. The black woman is not mad; she only wants to bring sanity to a somewhat crazy world. The "angry black woman" stereotype is nothing but a label invented by society to silence women of color who are unsatisfied with the partiality society gives us.

Chapter Eleven

Black Girl Magic or Black Girl Failure

Sojourner Truth, Harriet Tubman, Maya Angelou, Cicely Tyson, Mary McLeod Bethune, Mae Jemison, Zora Neale Hurston, Fannie Lou Hamer, Madam C.J. Walker, Michelle Obama, and Ruby Bridges. - #BlackGirlMagic

I often scroll through social media, and I see the hashtag "BlackGirlMagic" on several posts (even on some of my personal friends' pages). It made me think about how much black girl magic we are positively depicting, or if the black girl magic movement within our race is instilling false cultural ideals. And what I mean by false cultural ideals is this: how can you say "Black girl magic" but are dying your skin light, wearing a weave, wearing makeup to contour your natural "black" features, wearing large false lashes...in essence, giving a false perception of who you are as black women.

There are women who scream "Black girl magic" because they are making major contributions to the community, but have also gotten butt implants, breast implants, nose jobs, and lip work to personify another culture. To me, this screams what I call "Black girl failure." When you are in the community amongst young women who are not only listening but are also watching, you are directly falsifying a reality (even if it is to endorse a product to make money or a business to raise it).

It is no secret that social media opened Pandora's box when it comes to self-esteem and acceptance. We should be molding and setting strong cultural values for those who are paying attention instead of confusing ideals of self-love with representations of self-hate. As a society, we are failing them and others by personifying this stigma, indicating that the only way they represent Black girl magic is if they have long straight hair, big butts, fake lashes, long nails, thin waist, lots of money, etc.; instead of teaching self-love beginning within and loving (and embracing) what is seen outward. People excuse that thought because all that matters is that they are achieving personal success. Good looks are amazing to have. I mean, everyone covets that "pretty privilege," after all, but there are things more important than pretty, and these are the things we should give a higher priority to. There is so much more power in our actions than in our words.

At what point do we turn back the clock, where we instill loving ourselves with the features and figures of our ancestors instead of removing all of the features that made other cultures envious? Black women, we are instilling in our youth that this is not acceptable to have those features and be successful or to fit in. We are failing the youth and immature adults (let's be honest, age is a number and does not indicate maturity) by presenting to the world false ideals of black representation, and, let's face it, representation matters! There have been higher rates of suicide amongst African American youth over the last few years, and some in part because they do not accept or embrace their skin color the way they should. They are mocked and teased into harming themselves. All because of societal pressures to be a certain way, look a certain way, or act a certain way.

Our ancestors were strong. Our ancestors had power. Our ancestors were bold. They made power moves while not having to change or conform to look like someone else. The women mentioned in the very beginning of this chapter made a difference without disfiguring their natural-born beauty; even though they met with ridicule, slander, and mocking about their color and their features. They excelled and continued to perform while making lasting differences in our history. They did not forsake their values or principles to fit into societal socialization changes.

I have found myself in deep thought and reflection as to how I could have possibly failed those who look to me or look up to me as a role model or for some kind of positive encouragement. Yes, you see a very strong. Inspiring and "unapologetically" living woman today, but I promised myself to be honest about my past (after all, it has grown me to be who I am today) and build healthy boundaries to ensure the energy around me is promoting healthy self-love. Quite honestly, only the last seven or eight years have been awakening and life-accepting for me. Before then, what people saw was out of the pleasure of others. Though vain to a fault, I still allowed so many other people's opinions of me to influence how I felt about myself.

Media Hype

In a world growing with social media platforms and the number of likes indicating acceptance, it is time we throw caution to the wind and reel in our youth to understand reality and false truths. I want to note that I am by no means indicating that everything people post is a lie. What I am saying (and directly stating as fact) is that there are social media pages that have falsified information or are based merely on opinion.

I am also a FIRM believer that all of your personal business and every step you take should not be featured on social media. And yes, I understand it is "your" page, so you post "whatever you want;" however, I would like to reiterate that fact that how we represent ourselves online is being watched by youth (especially teenagers). Indirectly, we have to take some responsibility for how we are seen by those who are growing and dependent upon social media as an outlet for esteem, acceptance, and positive ways to grow to love themselves and others. Let's be honest: social media is a way to make money, and the youth are the best at this (not taking away from adults who have found ways to make money or make more money from the World Wide Web). Everyone wants to make money and enjoy the fancy things life has to offer, but what about a lasting legacy for others to see? What about a positive contribution to the Black legacy? We can talk of great women who are heroes of our time because of how hard they have fought for a worthy representation of color. We live in an era where we can lend our voices to a greater cause of self-acceptance, black love, and everything that makes us great. To do this, we need to stop acting like the same people who oppress us, thinking it will lead to acceptance into their circle...it won't.

It is important to, at a minimum, start to change the narrative of what is considered influential on social media. Our youth are so hungry for likes and attention that they forget how to protect and respect one another and themselves. When I see young girls engaging in an unladylike fashion because of what they see media personalities do, it makes me cringe. I feel as if it is setting back the movement a lot of Black women have painstakingly made over the years to advocate for our respect. I am all for women freely expressing themselves and accepting their bodies, but if the only talent they have is twerking or being naked, they need to look deeper and find something more meaningful because that shit gets old.

The other ugly truth is that some of our youth are lost. So lost, a young girl can get jumped in the bathroom while being recorded instead of someone stepping in to break it up or go for help. Who is to blame? Young mothers who are as toxic as they are? Or television shows that promote animosity between Black women and make situations like that look entertaining. Well, it is not when it comes to the impact on our girls.

How does one begin to learn the importance of morality when it is not as present on television (especially on these female reality television shows) or on social media? Then we wonder why our youth are "broken." Instead of uplifting one another, they are jealous or envious. It is time to turn back the clocks. It takes a village, but we need to change how the village acts.

Unhealthy Values

Growing up, I was taught how to take care of myself. I was shown how to be a strong and independent thinker. I was shown the value of education and hard work. I was shown how not to live my life dependent on a man. But guess what? I was also shown how to care for a man. I was shown how to submit to man. I was shown how to find value in a man (and not monetarily). I was shown how to love a man. I was taught how to nurture, period.

Over the last decade (or two), I feel as though we are raising headstrong, independent-thinking young ladies; however, we are not raising young ladies to focus on their personal lives. Yes, Black women, we are moving up in the world and doing magnificent things. We are working moms, corporate leaders, doctors, lawyers, professors, politicians...we are go-getters. We are fighting for equal pay, equal medical care, and the right to make decisions about our bodies. GOT IT! I fight and advocate for all of those things, too. But times have changed, and, in those changes, our family values have, too. And not always in the best way.

I am sure you are looking quite baffled about what I just said, given that I have spent time in this book writing about focusing on my professional and academic life and ignoring my personal life. It is very true. I did...mentally and emotionally. But you know what? When I was a wife (and even a girlfriend), there was never a time I did not physically cater to my man (to a certain degree, of course). By cater, I mean traditional roles (cooking, making his plate, cleaning, doing laundry, etc.). Trust me, in return, I had traditional expectations of my own (opening doors, taking out the trash, cleaning, paying for dinner if we went out, sending me flowers, and other chivalrous things). No, I am not trying to set women back 100 years. I am merely pointing out the importance of balance in a relationship and its give and take. It should not be something to be expected, but something naturally given. Essentially, what I am saying is that we need to teach young ladies how to pursue their dreams and give healthy space to relationships. They do not have to choose to have one or the other to be happy. They can make life decisions that can help the two coexist to make them become better friends, girlfriends, wives, and mothers.

One last thing. We need to teach our young ladies the value of therapy and self-care. As my cousin, Ashley McGirt (who is also known as the popular millennial therapist), says, "Self-care is not going to get your hair or nails done. That is basic hygiene." Self-care is making time to pause, reflect, and breathe. It is about mental and emotional wellness. We don't advocate enough for it, and it is needed in our community of dynamic women forcing themselves to do all and be all. It is not easy, and we all need to be representatives of realness and authenticity. And that means being honest with what we put out to the world.

The moment we realize that we, as Black women, have so much unspeakable power to influence and inspire others, we show how comfortable we are in our skin and love our other unique features. We send a message of how conscious we are of who we are and what we represent. We constantly make contributions and deserve all the success we get and the accomplishments we attain in society just by being ourselves.

THAT is Black Girl Magic.

Chapter Twelve

Social Stigmas = False Realities

"Social stigmas thrive when we accept illusions as truth. The courage to question false realities is the first step toward authentic freedom." – Dr. P. Gurley

Have you ever seen a grown, golden, melanin woman walk by with a sexy and confident strut, head high, back straight, hair neatly in place, and slaying in an outfit? I am sure the answer is yes. Now here comes the real question: what is the first perception of her that crosses your mind when you see her? What are your thoughts? Is it:

She looks arrogant.

She thinks she's all that. She is Bougie.

She does not look submissive. She is unapproachable.

She is egotistical.

She's cute, but I bet she can't cook.

Sadly, all of these perceived notions have been said about me by people who have either never said a word to me or told me these things after we became friends. I am sure there are a lot of women who can relate to this or, quite possibly, be guilty of making these same judgments. Why? Because no matter how far we move forward as a society, black women continue to have a much more difficult time escaping social stigmas placed upon them.

As a self-aware black woman who has always been outrightly focused on achieving my goals and hell-bent on attaining what I consider success in my career (academic or business), I have hardly fit into the picture of what an ideal black woman should be. But why not? I know what I want and will not accept anything short of it. But this is not how I have been perceived, and quite honestly, this shit is tiring and really played out. It's not hidden news that statistically, black women are outpacing their male peers in earning college degrees, starting businesses, and closing crucial voting margins. And you know what, I think this is an absolutely beautiful thing. I love knowing more women are getting out there doing what they love and fucking killing it - even against what feels like impossibilities and social disapproval by detractors and proving that they can achieve their goals and defy the odds against them. THIS is how a narrative changes. OR NOT!

False realities represent a notion of social characteristics appearing to be true but aren't. Women all over the world, but particularly black women, are victims of social stigmatization in the way we dress, the words we use, the way we wear our hair, the way we walk, and/or if we decide to show overt sexuality. The media, especially on television and in movies, have helped in shaping the context of black women, where reality shows and movie scripts are deliberately written or edited to make Black women appear stubborn, conceited, aggressive, ignorant, undomesticated, and loud. Black women are not the only ones known to be this way or make outbursts on and off the television, so why attribute the majority of the negative social stigmas to us?

Again, representation matters, and the media should be cautious about how the representation of black women is portrayed to avoid misinforming a society driven by social presence and social pressure. Yes,

I get it. Sex sells, as does drama. But our ancestral cultural values, as well as how far we have come as double minorities, should be considered to not only correct but also change the narrative of negative perceptions against black women. And to all the black queens reading this, as women, we tend to quickly forget how priceless we are and how important it is to love ourselves in a society that tends to vilify us and pit us against each other. We need to be more intentional when it comes to one another. We need to be more intentional when it comes to ourselves. I can never stress enough how important self-love and self-acceptance are, especially if you are a young black woman growing up in this age of technology and internet bullying.

How we identify ourselves with the world is so important for healthy thinking and healthy living. Equally, how we are represented to the world is also important. It is easy to judge others when you are not in their shoes. It is easy to point fingers when you are not in their position. It is easy to dismiss a confident young black woman as standoffish or stuck-up. What you don't know is how hard it was for her or what she has been through that has made her decide to rise above all the social stigmas. It is certainly what happened to me.

I feel like my life was a mess in my 20s and early 30s. I cannot say it was all a bad mess, because I had a lot of fun. I just ignored or accepted things I should not have. By my mid-30s, though, I felt like a new me. I found freedom from my negative thoughts. Freedom from my need to fit in. Freedom of my presence to others. Freedom. At this point, I had a very different perspective on race relations, how I felt about myself, and how others saw me. This perspective was fostered by embracing who I was as a woman first (which starts inside) and also having five nieces who are on all spectrums of melanin beauty. Most importantly, I refused to be defined by what I looked like on the outside and recognized the strength that comes along with the melanin that flows through my veins. Character is not built on outward beauty. Character is built on who we allow ourselves to become and what we advocate for. I believe we are all made beautiful, but we need to understand it is more than that. It is more than "skin deep." And that is the only reality that matters.

Chapter Thirteen

Sisterhood as a Sanctuary

"Sisterhood is the sacred space where our stories are safe, our dreams are encouraged, and our hearts are held without judgment." - Dr. P. Gurley

For so long, the world has told Black women that strength is a solitary pursuit. We are praised for our independence, our ability to "handle it," our capacity to carry the weight of our families, our communities, and ourselves. What I have learned, and what I continue to learn, is that true strength is found in the sanctuary of sisterhood. It is in the spaces where we are seen, heard, and held by other women who understand the unique contours of our journey.

Sisterhood is not just a buzzword or a social media hashtag. It is a lifeline, a source of healing, joy, and collective power. My own journey has been shaped by the women who have walked beside me, who have challenged me, inspired me, and reminded me that I am never alone. In a world that often pits us against each other, sisterhood is a radical act of resistance.

I think of the mentors who poured into me when I was just starting out, women who saw my potential before I could see it in myself. They taught me that success is not a zero-sum game and that there is enough room at the table for all of us. Their encouragement gave me the confidence to take risks, to speak up, and to claim my space. Their example taught me to reach back and lift others as I climb.

There have been friendships that sustained me through heartbreak, disappointment, and loss. We have laughed together, cried together, and celebrated each other's wins as if they were our own. In those moments, I learned that vulnerability is not a liability but a gift. When we share our stories, our struggles, and our dreams, we create a tapestry of connection that is stronger than any individual thread.

Sisterhood is also about accountability. The women in my life have loved me enough to tell me the truth, even when it was hard to hear. They have challenged me to grow, to confront my blind spots, and to become a better version of myself. Their honesty is a mirror that reflects both my strengths and my areas for growth. In their presence, I am free to be fully myself—flawed, evolving, and worthy of love.

Creating safe spaces for Black women is one of the most important things we can do. Whether it is a book club, a group chat, a professional network, or a quiet conversation over coffee, these spaces are sanctuaries where we can exhale. They are places where we can lay down the armor, shed the masks, and rest in the knowledge that we are understood. In these spaces, we don't have to explain ourselves or justify our existence. We can simply be.

Sisterhood is not always easy. It requires intention, vulnerability, and a willingness to work through conflict. There have been times when jealousy, competition, or misunderstanding threatened to fracture relationships. I have learned that true sisterhood is built on forgiveness, empathy, and a commitment to growth. We are stronger together, not in spite of our differences, but because of them.

I am committed to creating and sustaining spaces where Black women can thrive. I believe in the power of collaboration over competition, of sharing resources and opportunities, of celebrating each other's achievements. When one of us wins, we all win. When one of us is hurting, we all feel it. This is the essence of sisterhood, a shared destiny and a collective rising.

If you are longing for deeper connection, know that you are not alone. Reach out. Start the conversation. Be the friend, the mentor, the sister you wish you had. It does not take a grand gesture. Sometimes it is a text, a smile, a listening ear. Sometimes it is showing up, even when you do not have the right words. Sometimes it is simply holding space for someone else's story.

Sisterhood is not about perfection. It is about presence. It is about choosing, every day, to show up for each other—to celebrate, to support, to challenge, and to love. It is about building a legacy of connection that will outlast us all. As I look around at the women in my life, I am filled with gratitude. For the laughter, the wisdom, the courage, and the grace. For the ways we hold each other up and call each other higher. For the sanctuary we create together; a place where we are free to be fully ourselves.

May this chapter be an invitation to seek out, nurture, and cherish the sisterhoods in your own life. May you find sanctuary in the company of women who see you, who love you, and who remind you that you are never alone. Because together, we are unstoppable.

Chapter Fourteen

Socially Conscious

A strong black woman is what I am, what I will always be...in my blood and in my soul. That is something no one can change." - Dr. P. Gurley

Let me reiterate the fact that I have never forsaken the fact that I was a "black girl," but what became more apparent was how differently people began to treat me (especially in my own community of "like" women). By "like" women, I have to admit, I have never surrounded myself with women who were not pushing to achieve some level of personal success (whether in business or academics). At least, that is what I thought until those relationships went south due to jealousy, envy, or complacency (theirs, not mine). In my mind, I wondered, "What was so different about me that made other women uncomfortable, distant, or not like me?" It is not in my nature to say that all women are jealous, but what I will say is that women who dislike other women they do not know or do not have a reason not to like is a direct reflection of how they feel about themselves (which let's face it, is a form of self-hatred, envy, and/or jealousy). In saying that, let me also say this: it is not pleasurable to be a victim of your natural, God-given features, talents, or gifts. Unfortunately, this is something you cannot control, but you can control how you think and feel about yourself.

When you live a rich life (not in the financial sense), you worry less about others' opinions of you. You worry less about how others relate to you. You live with a sense of purpose and passion. Living a rich life entails having that peace of mind so much that you are living your own life and do not have time to be in-tune with someone else or allow someone else to be in-tune with yours (in a decision-making way). I am not a person of controversy, and there was a time when I worried more about how others felt, to the point of neglecting my own feelings. Then I had to ask myself, "Who am I living for?" and better yet, "Why do I care more about his/her perspective or opinion of me than I do my own?"

There comes a time in your life when you have to come to peace with the decisions you have made. Then and only then can you reflect on why those decisions were made and who those decisions really belonged to or were for. Were they really for you? Or were they for someone else? Where is the peace in living for someone else? And where is your peace while you are living for others? Let me state this disclaimer: By no means am I a clinical or licensed psychologist, but I have mentored and counseled many who have spent a great deal of their lives living for others. I was guilty of it myself at one time.

So, back to the people who feel they are at liberty to inject their opinion into your life. No longer let them. If you ever want to quiet them, simply ask, "Is your backyard clean or dirty?" If you opened their closet, what would fall out? YOUR life does not require explanations when YOU are living it. A part of life is learning, and sometimes learning hurts. Most times, learning experiences make you stronger. I find it easier to deal with the hurt if I am the one making decisions. First, you stop blaming others and place the blame where it belongs...on you. Second, when you are at peace, the decisions you make are clearer, and you are able to discern between compromise, humbleness, and actually "pleasing someone." The only person in life you can control is you. You control your actions; you control how you allow others to treat you; you control how others see you, etc. And as far as I am concerned, controlling myself is enough to not have peace of mind on any given day...lol. Why add to losing all of my peace of mind by adding someone else's opinion of me to that?

There is one area in life that requires a balance, and it consists of the desire to be both humble and selfless, all while being selfish. I know it seems strange to use the word selfish in such a sense when talking about being both humble and selfless; however, life can never be as simple or easy as we would like. And personally speaking, it takes a special kind of ability to be this way. The purpose of accepting selfishness as a positive is to develop the ability to love others while not placing others before yourself. Self-love is favoring your joy, happiness, and comfort over someone else's. It is being in a constant state of self-worth.

I want you to understand that none of this means you are not willing to compromise, as I find it important to broaden your horizons by trying new things, going to new places, or not being fearful of failing at something or worrying about not being good at something. What I am stating is that when you love yourself, you are able to open yourself to possibilities without putting your emotions, feelings, thoughts, comforts, or regard on the back burner. Women are very nurturing and instantly want to please, and sometimes without thought. How many times has a friend, or your significant other, called wanting you to do something or want to talk, and you REALLY are not in the mood? But guess what, you do it anyway, without a single reservation or thought to please another person. Have you ever given thought to being honest and asked yourself, "Is this life or death, and can this wait?" or do you simply roll with punches and then feel some kind of way because you REALLY needed that moment for yourself (especially after a long day)? I have to admit I am guilty of rolling with the punches at times; however, my decisions to do so are consciously made. Yep, I consciously make the decision to do things with other people (and more than people may realize). I actually give careful thought to my actions before I react to them or act on them. People make poor decisions when in a pleasing mode with no thoughtful perspective of the situation or issue. Believe me, I am not saying this is a bad thing; what I am saying is to consider and weigh each situation (even if for 10 seconds). If you put a timer on for 10 seconds, there is sufficient time to breathe and briefly reflect while exhaling. At that moment, your gut instantly answers for you. Now, whether you listen to it or not is up to you. As with everything I am sharing in this book, it is my truth. And my truth makes me H.E.R.

So, how do you begin to love yourself? Gosh, this can be so different for everyone, and this is what makes each person unique. There is one area that is not so unique. It is the area of acceptance. Accept where you are in your life. Accept the decisions you made in the past that got you to this point in your life. Accept that you cannot change the past, but you can learn and grow from it. Reflect on the things you would do differently now. What can you take from those situations that you can use as you move forward? Do not hang on to these things if they are negative, nor if you feel guilty, bitter, or regretful about them. Simply accept your life and your circumstances (good or bad), and make the decision to take care of YOU. So, for now, do something good for you. Do not let this be a purchase (although retail therapy is a nice-to-do), but allow it to evoke an act of self-love. Do something out of the ordinary. If the weather is beautiful, let your imagination run wild and do what you would least expect. Be conscious. Be present. Be socially aware. Be intentional when you live, breathe, work, and love.

Postface

I t is not every day people make a conscious decision to openly write about pieces of their life (especially the most traumatic ones), and for me, it was even harder to make the decision to publish it for the world to read. Although it was not the easiest decision, this experience and the level of writing it required were therapeutic for me. It had been years since I was able to reflect on my past and realize how far I had come mentally, emotionally, spiritually, academically, professionally, and physically.

There is nothing more debilitating in life than feeling as if you do not have any control over it. YOU DO! All of it as it pertains to you. You have a gut...listen to it. Follow it! Believe it! Do not ignore this. And if you have to ask someone whether you should do something or not, most of the time, you already know. You just needed validation of what you felt. Yes, I have been there and used to spend a lot of time and energy asking people to make decisions for my life because I was too afraid of making them for myself, simply out of fear. And if something...no, when something did not go right, there was always someone else to blame. This is why it is liberating to live the life you want, putting healthy boundaries in place to protect your energy and your space.

I didn't do this soon enough in my life, but I hope this book gives you the courage and inspiration to recognize that you can live for yourself and be happy. Also, you do not have to be "boxed in" because someone else wants to place you in a category you feel is unbecoming and does not define who you are. Hell, you don't have to be "boxed in" because society tries to make it that way. Take the time to reflect and own who you are, and do so unapologetically.

Thank you for taking the time to hear my truth; now it is time to find yours. And if you already have it, continue to live in it. Life is better that way.

MY life...I unapologetically live.

MY thoughts...I unapologetically think.

MY decisions...I unapologetically make.

MY love...I unapologetically give.

My wellness...I unapologetically protect.

And you should too!

I AM H.E.R. (A Poem)

I am not a stereotype, I am **HER.**

Hero among the thieves that want to rob me of my identity, forsake me because of my ancestry, and change me because of my complexity.

Electric because I radiate a passion not understood by many. A magnetic force from birth; I was created in the image of warriors before me.

Rhythmic like a symphony, for my expressions are many.

Jazzy, soulful, Rhapsodic, and poetic.

I am not a stereotype, I am **HER.**

Humble to maintain the character traits of women who successfully rose with dignity, integrity, and morality.

Elegant because my skin will never define me the way my grace does.

Light skin, dark skin, brown skin...it's all sophisticated melanin.

Resilient in thought and practice because I tasted ambition at birth on my way from the womb.

I am not a stereotype, I am **HER.**

Happy to be me in a world of prejudice and racial injustice that tries to condemn me because of melanin.

Energetic because my power and stamina are needed to never cease progressing,

Reflective, for the decisions of my past are a remembrance of my growth and evolution.

I am not a stereotype, I am **HER.**

Hopeful to continue to live a life of perfect imperfection while never ceasing in my purpose.

Enterprising because sometimes blind faith is better than being scared.

Reliant on my aspirations of greatness to keep me sane when I begin to feel overwhelmed and nervous.

I am not a stereotype, I am **HER.**

Hedonic for my body was made to experience pain and pleasure fulfilled by sexual wit,

Erotic in the way I swing my hips, bat my eyes, and lick my lips.

Romantic because it is the secret of keeping the spark of black love lit.

I am not a stereotype, I am **HER.**

High reaching because I learned early in life to work hard, dream big, and never settle.

Experienced in many things, from interior decorating to teaching to speaking.

Resourceful in knowing where, knowing how, and most of all, knowing when to push the pedal to the metal.

I am not a stereotype, I am **HER.**

Heroic because my ancestors paved the way for me with their lives and against all odds,

Extraordinary because I am educated, a veteran, a Civil Servant, a CEO, an entrepreneur, a professor, a poet, a writer, a daughter, sister, aunt, mother, lover, and a friend.

Resolute because all I am and all I am to become is a reflection of my purpose, my destiny, and my legacy, because I am a faith-filled child of God.

I AM NOT A STEREOTYPE, I AM HER!

Self-Reflection Q&A

Being honest with yourself, take a moment to reflect on your life. Are you living in your truth?

What does it mean to you to live in your truth?

If you have gone natural, how did you feel about yourself (emotionally and mentally) as you went through the process (especially if you did the big chop)? How do you feel now?

How do you feel the world sees women with natural hair?

What would you change about yourself or your life that could positively influence the world around you?

Have you taken control of the direction of your life and your decisions? Why or why not?

Are you letting matters that are out of your control change the way you live? What can you do to change this?

Who is on your pedestal? Why are they there? If not you, why aren't you there?

What does self-care mean to you? What do you do to take care of yourself?

If you could write a letter to the person you were 10 years ago, what would it say?

Acknowledgments

There are so many people I would like to acknowledge, so please forgive me if you are not personally recognized in this book. You are all very near and dear to my heart.

First, I would like to acknowledge my cousin, Ashley McGirt. Though we did not get to co-author this publication together as planned, you are a constant contributor to my inspiration.

To my very dynamic, empowering, and inspirational friend, Tinisha Agramonte. I am grateful for your support and encouragement in my writing career, as well as for our friendship.

To my longtime friend, Kim Nelson. There are no words to describe the impact you have had on my life. You have taught me to be a better friend and believer in unconditional love, strength, happiness, and, most of all, how to experience joy through pain. I am thankful and blessed to call you a friend.

To all of my amazingly supportive friends, thank you for always encouraging and inspiring me from the moment we met and keeping me sane during many of the times I wanted to give up.

About the Author

D r. Pamela Gurley is a world-renowned author, speaker, and passionate literacy advocate who believes in the transformative power of words. As the founder of Clark and Hill Enterprise, IAMDRPGURLEY, and the Brown Girl and Brown Boy Literacy Foundation, she dedicates her work to empowering children and adults to find their voice, embrace their stories, and break barriers through education.

With a Doctorate in Management and a background in psychology and administration, Dr. Gurley brings both expertise and lived experience to her mission. Her initiatives—including the Brown Girl and Brown Boy Kid's Red-Carpet Book Tour and the Literacy Festival—have inspired thousands and sparked meaningful change in communities nationwide.

Beyond her advocacy, Dr. Gurley is known for her authenticity and her ability to connect with audiences of all ages. Whether she is hosting the Herspiration Happy Hour podcast, leading a workshop, or writing her next book, she shows up as her whole self: relatable, driven, and unapologetically real.

Dr. Gurley's journey is proof that you can rewrite your story at any stage of life. Her mission is simple: to help others stand tall in their truth and live a life of purpose on purpose.

Other Books By Dr. Pamela Gurley

- I am Not a Stereotype: I Am H.E.R.

- Bl@ck Girl Activist: Changing the Narrative of Black Women

- The PR Prep Guide: 7 Critical Need-To-Know Basics Before Hiring a Publicist

- Bl@ck Girl Activist: A Shift in Social Change (Anthology)

- The Dream is in Her Hands: She Can Do It (Anthology)

- The Pedestal Philosophy: Your Pedestal. Your Power. Your Truth.

Children's Books:

English:

- Brown Boy Be Social

- Brown Girl, Be Social

- Brown Girl, Break Barriers

- Brown Boy, Break Barriers

- Brown Girl, and Brown Boy, Be Well

- Brown Girl and Brown Boy, Be Mindful

- Brown Girl and Brown Boy, We Love Hobbies

- Brown Girl and Brown Boy, Africa Adventures

- Brown Girl and Brown Boy Presents Kofi Roux the Yorkiepoo

Spanish:

- Niña Morena, Sé Sociable

- Niño Moreno, Sé Sociable

- Niña Morena, Rompe Barreras

- Niño Moreno, Rompe Barreras

- Niña Morena y Niño Moreno, Manténganse Saludables

- Niña Morena y Niño Moreno, Sean Considerables

- Niña Morena y Niño Moreno, Nos Encantan Los Pasatiempos

French:

- Petite Fille Noire, Sois Sociable

- Petit Garçon Noir, Sois Sociable

- Petit Garçon Noir, Brises Barrières

- Petite Fille Noire, Brises Barrières

- Petite Fille Noire et Petit Garçon Noir, Soyez Prévenants

- Petite Fille Noire et Petit Garçon Noir, Allez Bien!

- Petite Fille Noire et Petit Garçon Noir, Nous Aimons des Loisirs